Genealogy Basics Online

A Step-by-Step Introduction to Finding Your Ancestors Through the Internet

Cherri Melton Flinn

Genealogy Basics Online

Library of Congress Catalog Number: 99-068483

ISBN: 1-9296850-0-9

5   4   3   2   1

Educational facilities, companies, and organizations interested in multiple copies or licensing of this book should contact the publisher for quantity discount information. Training manuals, CD-ROMs, and portions of this book are also available individually or can be tailored for specific needs.

MUSKA&LIPMAN

Muska & Lipman Publishing
2645 Erie Avenue, Suite 41
Cincinnati, Ohio 45208
www.muskalipman.com
publisher@muskalipman.com

This book is composed in Berkeley, Univers, and Printers' Ornaments typefaces using QuarkXpress 4.1, Adobe Photoshop 5.0.2, and Adobe Illustrator 8.0. Created in Cincinnati, Ohio, in the United States of America.

Credits

Publisher
Andy Shafran

Managing Editor
Hope Stephan

Editorial Services Manager
Elizabeth A. Agostinelli

Content Editor
Kate Maloy

Proofreader
Caroline Roop

Cover Designer
Dave Abney

Production Manager
Cathie Tibbetts

Production Team
DOV Graphics
   Michelle Frey
   Stephanie Japs
   Tammy Norton
   John Windhorst

Indexer
Kevin Broccoli

Printer
Von Hoffmann Graphics

About the Author

Cherri Melton Flinn is an Illinois-based freelance writer and instructor. Fascinated by genealogy since childhood, she began pursuing her interest several years ago on the Internet, only to be frustrated by seeing the many possibilities, yet finding little in the way of guidance on how to use what was available. As she puts it, "Finding the family history Web sites is easy; finding *your* family history is another story." Her husband gave her search a big boost when he gave her a family tree software package for her birthday. Soon she was helping other people in her hometown of 11,000, as family and friends began calling on her for advice as they attempted to build their own family trees. Cherri began teaching a class on genealogy on the Internet at a local community college, and the class filled the first time it was offered. Given the high level of interest and the lack of adequate instructional materials, she decided to write this book. She has since been recruited to offer workshops on the topic at another local college near her home.

Dedication

This book is dedicated to the strong branches and roots that are a part of my family tree. I am so fortunate and proud to be a part of this wonderful family!

Husband, Mike, and children Erin, Jason and Kevin

Parents Jim and Dixie Melton
　　　　Raymond and Margaret Flinn

Jim, Jayne, Matt, Megan & Tyler Melton

Sue and Jim Collins

Acknowledgments

I would like to thank all of the Muska & Lipman team. It's been a wonderful experience and I appreciate all of the time and effort you have put into this project. Special thanks to Andy Shafran, Hope Stephan, and Kate Maloy for all of your insight and enthusiasm.

Thanks to Judy for your encouragement and support!

Thank you, Herb Russell.

Thank you to Charles Swinney for your kind words that encouraged me to finish this book.

Table of Contents

Introduction

How long have you been looking for the roots and branches of your family tree? It doesn't matter whether you have spent years researching family history or just want to begin—this book will be your guide. By following the four steps in this book, you will find people and facts that you never knew existed!

In the past few years, many books about conducting genealogy research on the World Wide Web have hit the market. Unfortunately, most are merely collections of Web sites, offering little or no instruction about how to navigate the Internet.

Throughout this book, you will see countless references to the Internet and the World Wide Web. Many people use the terms interchangeably, but in actuality they mean two different things. The Web is a collection of interlinked documents. The Internet is the interactive, global association of computers capable of communicating with one another.

The World Wide Web gives Internet users the ability to point with their mouse, click on a link, and be rapidly transported to a specific Web page. Before the invention of the Web, you had to type in the exact Internet address of where you wanted to go. In simplest terms, think of the Internet as the "information superhighway" that makes transporting data possible. The World Wide Web is the "express lane" on that highway, which allows you to reach your destination quickly.

How This Book Will Help You

What sets this book apart is its simplicity. *Genealogy Basics Online* gently guides the reader through the Internet and provides all of the tools necessary for helping anyone succeed in finding family history information on the Internet. I developed this method after teaching classes on this subject and learning that nearly all my students were at different points in their knowledge of genealogy and computers. I address those differences through the book's four easy steps. Don't be surprised if you find family connections online at the first or second Web site you visit.

Here is the key to using this book: Read each Web site's description, because most descriptions contain instructions for successfully navigating and searching that particular site. The tips and recommendations throughout this book are true timesavers, resulting in more productive searches.

If you have been using the Internet for some time and are still unfamiliar with Web browsers, search engines, and URLs, then it's time to upgrade your skills. Understanding how Web directories are arranged and how search engines work gives the average Web surfer an edge when it comes to finding information online.

Keep this book by your computer and refer to it often. It will assist you in every aspect of your genealogy research. Enjoy your journey!

Conventions Used in This Book

As you read through the sections that follow, you will find several conventions for highlighting specific types of information that you'll find especially useful:

Tip
Text formatted in this manner offers extra information related to the issue being discussed. You'll find personal anecdotes and experiences, specific techniques, and general information extras in "Tip" boxes.

Note
A "Note" introduces information that is interesting, or might help you avoid problems, but is not necessarily essential to the discussion. Notes also offer advice relating to a specific topic.

Caution
A "Caution" box describes actions and commands that could make irreversible changes to your files or cause problems in the future. It might also highlight possible security concerns. Make sure you read this material carefully, because the information it contains could directly affect your files, software, or hardware or result in other unwanted consequences.

All World Wide Web addresses (called URLs) are in **boldface**.

Let's get started!

Step 1

Getting Organized

Gather and organize as much information as you can about your family history—before you venture onto the Web. If you have already done this, proceed to Step 2. Otherwise, follow this procedure.

SECTION ONE:
Compile Your Records

Start by recording everything you know, because the more you have on hand, the easier your online research will be. For each person in your family tree, try to gather all the information listed below:

◆ Name (last, first, and middle names; maiden name, if female)

◆ Birthday (month/day/year)

◆ Birthplace (city and state; hospital, if possible)

◆ Death date (month/day/year)

◆ Cause of death (coroner's report)

◆ Burial place (city, state, cemetery)

◆ Marriage (month/day/year; [maiden] name of spouse; city, state, church)

◆ Divorce, if any (date; city and state where filed)

◆ Ethnicity

◆ Religion (churches attended)

◆ Occupation(s)

◆ Military service records

◆ Place(s) of residence

◆ Medical history (genetic diseases, if any)

◆ Parents and children*

   *As with everything else, gather as much detail as possible, being sure to record birth dates and death dates.

This might seem like a lot of information to compile, but the more you know, the easier and faster your search will be. The rewards will belong not only to you but also to future generations—your nieces, nephews, children, and *their* children. In essence, you will be creating history by recording it. Accuracy is crucial. Use a Family Group Sheet to keep a careful record for each branch of your family tree—that is, for each family connected to your own.

Right now, you might be wondering, "Where am I going to find all this stuff?" Relax. *You are not going to find everything.* Yes, it *is* necessary to locate data, but don't become so obsessed with finding every bit of it that you miss the big picture. You are looking for just enough "glue" to bind your family history together.

Think of your personal genealogy research as a treasure hunt. If you get no further than talking to your parents or your grandparents, you will already have found the gold. Spend an afternoon with them, and you will surely discover things you never knew about them and about yourself. Write down more than facts and dates. Keep a record of anecdotes, events, relationships. Try to write a small biography of those people who mean so much to you and have influenced your life.

Most people own something that once belonged to a family member—a family heirloom or just a memento of someone special. Was it a pendant from Grandma? Granddad's pocket watch? There's probably a story that goes with it—*write it down*! Those are the stories that bring a family's history to life, making it exciting and unique. Remember, though, that you are not in the business of fabricating or embellishing stories. Be sure to get the details down accurately.

Everyone's life is different, which means everyone's stories contain different struggles, successes, and failures. It will be no small task to separate the facts from the fiction that many people weave into their accounts of important events. Just make sure you record the facts as facts and the stories as "family anecdotes" or "yarns." Personally, I have no problem with recording an unsubstantiated "story" in the family history, as long as future generations realize that it *is* unsubstantiated. They can draw their own conclusions or seek more information.

> *"A historian tells history.*
> *A genealogist tells his story."*
>
> —Anonymous quote from the Internet

Be sure to document the source of each piece of data that you record. This will save you time and frustration later on, and it could help you resolve any mismatches between your facts and those of someone else who may be researching your family or one of its branches. Careful documentation can prevent discrepancies and errors down the road. Avoid those obstacles!

Tip

Documentation is just the process of recording when and from whom you received a piece of information. If you gathered the data from books at a library or courthouse, you might have a photocopy. Here's an old trick! Every time you copy information from the pages of a book, make a copy of the book's title and copyright pages. Then make a copy of the book's cover and spine. Staple these to the front of the other material you have copied from that book. If you ever need to refer to the book again, you will know exactly what to look for, even if you are in another library.

Keep a contact or correspondence log, too, in which you write down every phone call and every letter you receive or send. Genealogists also document their cemetery research. When recording tombstone inscriptions, include every bit of information from the headstone, including the date of your visit to the cemetery, the name of the cemetery, and its exact location (so you can return if need be).

Don't forget: Document everything!

Now, start making plans to visit a few courthouses and cemeteries. In the meantime, look for what's closer to home. You may be surprised by the amount of information that's right at hand—but you never knew was genealogy-related.

There are many great genealogy books that can tell you how to conduct in-depth family research without using computers. Our purpose, however, is to help you use the Internet efficiently for your research, and Step 1 is meant to give you an overview of what you need to get started. Here is a fairly comprehensive checklist of information you can often find right at home:

CHECKLIST

◆ School papers/report cards (many have parents' signatures)

◆ Scrapbooks

◆ Yearbooks

◆ Personal letters, cards, correspondence

◆ Photographs (check the backs for any names, dates or locations)

◆ Personal phone and address books

◆ Journals or diaries

◆ Recipe files or recipe books

◆ Books (look for inscriptions)

◆ Family heirlooms (sometimes these come with letters or inscriptions)

You might think you can't possibly find all of this information at home. Well, maybe it's time to make a trip to Grandma's or visit your parents. They probably have what you don't. And what about Aunt Clara or Uncle Bob? You know, the people who went to every family reunion? Contact them! More than likely, someone in your family kept records of your family reunions.

The sooner you do this, the better. Tomorrow could be too late. I try to carry paper and pen with me so that when I get together with relatives I can write down the little things that they tell me rather than making a mental note of them. Ask your close, or even distant, relatives to lend you any documents they are willing to share, such as obituaries, wedding announcements, birth announcements—you get the picture.

N o t e

You don't need a computer to do family research, but having one gives you more than access to information—it can help you store, retrieve, and share your data, too. If your file cabinets are overflowing with documents, you can scan them. Easy-to-use desktop scanners are very affordable today. Sometimes they are even included in your PC purchase. Scanning documents and photographs preserves these precious records, which then take up far less space on your hard drive than on your shelf. You can scan just about anything you find in your genealogy research—fragile newspaper clippings, magazine articles, letters, old photos, marriage licenses, death certificates, and other legal documents—and then you can organize them. Once you have saved and sorted them on your computer, you can print them out to share or carry with you, any time you wish. You can also e-mail these items to others or insert them into a personal, electronic family history book.

Scanning is particularly useful if you want to save only part of a book or document, for example, an entry from a gazetteer, a photo from an old yearbook, or the front section of a family Bible, where births and deaths have been noted.

Scanning old photos can be especially valuable. With relatively affordable software, or even shareware, you can take a damaged or faded photo and restore its appearance.

A good guide to buying the right scanner for your needs and learning how to use its many features is *Scanner Solutions*, by Winston Steward (Muska & Lipman, ISBN 0-9662889-7-1).

If you feel comfortable borrowing documentation and memorabilia, keep them only as long as you must. Make photocopies of everything you can. This not only gives you actual documents to substantiate your family record, it also saves you the tedious process of handwriting the details of a document and then recording them somewhere else. Making copies is fairly inexpensive when you consider the convenience and security they provide. Most people don't pay attention to newspaper clippings, announcements, and other such items when someone passes away and their personal belongings are parceled out. Making copies ensures that you can validate your work and protect the accuracy and completeness of your records in the case of a house fire or other disaster.

A big stumbling block for some people is the need to obtain historical data from a family member with whom they have no contact. If you are at odds with a relative, or just live far away from that person, his or her information is still critical to your research. Perhaps other relatives can get the information for you. Use whatever resources are available to you. If you are on speaking terms with the relative in question, but not especially close, you might draft a form letter explaining the family history you need and mail the letter with a self-addressed, stamped envelope. Or you could write a note and attach a copy of a Family Group Sheet. Make it as easy as you can for your relative to cooperate.

N o t e

Even though medical information is a delicate subject for some people, it's always good to request it. As sensitively as possible, be persistent about recording any genetic diseases in particular. Future generations will be thankful for the knowledge—especially because many genetic diseases can now be treated, or their onset delayed, through modern medical technology.

SECTION TWO:
Organize Your Data

Your search will be more fun and more productive if you organize it well. I will present a few tips on getting your act together. The rest will be up to you. Most of us have an idea of what will work for us in general. This is your personal project, so arrange it and schedule it in the ways that work best for you. Remember, you can consider yourself organized as long as you can put your hands on the information you need when you need it. Without a doubt, keeping yourself organized will be the biggest challenge most of you will face. When I began my research, I purchased a portable metal file case that holds standard manila file folders. The case can be locked and is fairly secure from the elements—and little hands. If you have children, as I do, it's necessary to keep important papers out of their reach.

It is crucial to have a good workspace. You don't have to buy a new desk or file cabinet; you just have to set aside an area for nothing but genealogy materials. You will be amazed at how much you can accumulate in a short time. One of the problems that I ran into was not knowing which part of my family tree to research, so I have been searching every branch I am aware of. You need not go to this extreme for an enjoyable, productive exploration of your family history.

Regardless of how many family lines you are tracing, you will probably find it convenient, as I do, to sort your information into manila file folders labeled for each surname you are researching. Then, when you make a trip to do your research, you can just grab the appropriate manila folder and go.

This hobby should be enjoyable, and being organized makes it much easier to locate a specific piece of information. Ask any genealogist about rifling through hundreds of papers, looking for the birth date of an ancestor! Without organization, the research can become cumbersome, more like a job than a pleasant pastime.

You can organize all your research materials by putting your computer to work. Investing in family tree software for your computer will make filing and sorting your information a breeze. The software will assist you in ways that you never dreamed possible. Entering your research into the computer, instead of maintaining records by hand, will save you hours upon hours of time better spent on the research itself.

If you do not own a computer, you can still reap the benefits of the Internet in your genealogical research. What you *will* need is *access* to a computer that is connected to the Internet. This is becoming easier and easier as more and more schools and libraries connect to the World Wide Web. Many libraries, even in rural areas, now offer the use of computers with Internet access, often right next to the microfiche viewers or card catalogs. In the future, we may see computers with Internet access in *every* library.

Tip

In 1995, WebTV Networks, Inc. was founded. WebTV aims to be a user-friendly and affordable alternative avenue to the Internet. WebTV Internet units come equipped with a built-in Web browser and your television serves as a monitor for the system. Newer models have a built-in printer port that is compatible with select Hewlett-Packard and Canon printers.

Just like other Web browsers, the WebTV browser features searching capabilities, bookmarking of favorite sites, and an e-mail program. WebTV uses Infoseek as its search engine of choice, although you may access any of the search engines mentioned in this book. The unit has no storage capabilities, so you will not be able to install family tree software or store information to a floppy disk.

What you will be able to do is send and receive e-mail, search through all of the genealogy sites mentioned in this book, and print information from the Internet. Currently, WebTV is available in the United States, Canada, and Japan, with plans to expand the service to other countries. If you want to get on the Internet and are on a budget, consider WebTV as a viable option for searching your family history.

http://www.webtv.net

Figure 1.1
WebTV.

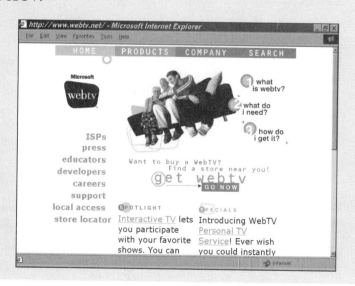

If you do own a computer, and you want to use it to organize your information, many software programs are available. Family Tree Maker and Generations are just two that can help you get started. On the Internet, you can go to the Web site at Family Tree Maker (located at this address: **http://www.familytreemaker.com**) and download a free—yes, I said *free*—trial version of *Family Tree Maker* (FTM). However, I am not in the business of endorsing specific software programs. This is a very individual matter. I suggest you explore several programs until you find one that you are comfortable with and that offers some technical support.

Advantages to any computerized family tree program include the option of exchanging family trees with other genealogists via the computer and also the opportunity to submit your tree to a large database, like the World Family Tree. The World Family Tree is a project undertaken by Family Tree Maker, where people can publish their family history on the Internet and invite contact with other family members worldwide. FTM is not the only software program that offers this. Here are the names of a few family tree programs, along with their Web site addresses.

◆ The Master Genealogist
   http://www.whollygenes.com

◆ Ultimate Family Tree
   http://www.uftree.com

◆ Family Tree Maker
   http://www.familytreemaker.com

◆ Cumberland Family Tree
   http://www.cf-software.com

◆ Legacy Family Tree
   http://www.legacyfamilytree.com

Tip

Buy family tree software at a discount. If you are interested in trying some of the new programs, but don't want to spend much money, try bidding on software at one of the online auction Web sites like eBay (**http://www.ebay.com**). eBay sellers usually have a steady supply of family tree software. Some of the software titles are the old versions, before the updated ones came out. On the auction sites, you can usually obtain the software for half what you would pay at the computer store or less. If you do buy an outdated version of a family tree program, check to see whether an upgrade is available. You might be able to buy the outdated program and the upgrade for less than the cost of the newest version at your local computer shop. So, newer isn't necessarily better. Do be sure that any software you buy is compatible with your computer. Check also to see whether the software is returnable; most computer stores are unwilling to accept returns. Lastly, if you want inexpensive genealogy materials (like books, forms, publications), the auctions on the Internet are the place to go. There is an overwhelming number of books on surnames, town histories, records, diaries, and other information that can help you in your research.

The programs listed above are just a few of those that I feel will serve the purpose for most family researchers. For a comprehensive list of software, go to Cyndi's List and look under the category Software (**http://www.cyndislist.com/ software.htm#Software**). Most of the free family tree programs are for demonstration only and will allow the user to enter only about twenty names. They are just trial sizes, but at least you can see how they operate. Read the directions that come with the program. The directions are usually found under a file called "Read Me." If you don't like the program, just uninstall or delete it. Once you experience the ease of managing your records with a computer program, you'll wonder how you ever did it the old-fashioned way.

Knowing how to download files properly is a big asset to anyone who does research. If you have never before downloaded anything from the Internet onto your computer, now is the time to learn. Follow this step-by-step guide.

1. When you find a text file or program that you want to download, there will be a box or icon somewhere on the Web site labeled Download. Click on this.

2. A dialog box will appear that looks something like Figure 1.2:

Figure 1.2

A File Download dialog box.

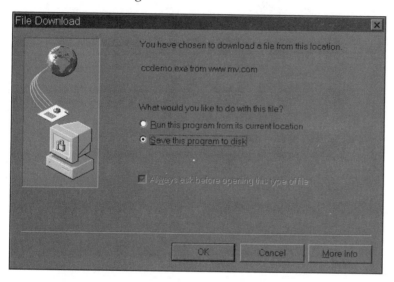

3. Click on the circle that says Save This File or Program to Disk, then click OK.

4. The Save As dialog box will appear. Click on the down arrow by the pull-down menu. You can save your file to any one of these locations by clicking on it: "Desktop," "My Computer," "3 1/2 Floppy," or "C Drive" (which is usually your computer's hard drive). For example, if you want to save the file on your hard drive, click on "C Drive." If folders are displayed, click on the folder in which you want to save this file. See Figure 1.3.

Figure 1.3

The Save As dialog box.

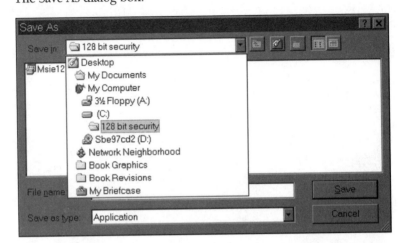

Usually, when you download a file or program from the Internet, a name will appear in the box titled File Name. If you want to rename the downloaded file, do it now. After the download is complete, you will need to be able to locate this file by name so you can open it.

Below the File Name box is the Save As box. The format of the file or program you are downloading from the Internet will be displayed here. If the file is all text, it will usually have a name and a suffix (or prefix) such as *.txt* or *.wpd*. For example, if the file name is *august.wpd*, "august" is the name of the file you are downloading and ".wpd" identifies it as a WordPerfect document. Corel WordPerfect is the name of a word processing program. If the file were a Microsoft Word processing program, ".doc" would be the suffix. The suffix always identifies the manner in which the document was saved.

5. Now, click the Save button to save your file or program. Another box will pop up (See Figure 1.4) and show the progress of the download. When the download is finished, another small box will appear, which says "Download Complete." Click OK in the dialog box to confirm the download's completion.

F i g u r e   1 . 4

The Downloading dialog box.

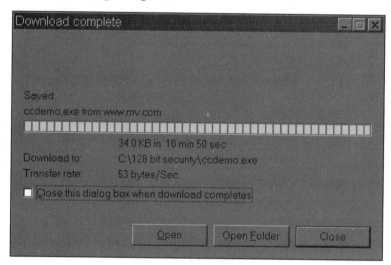

6. The downloaded file or program is now stored either on your computer's hard drive or on a floppy disk. If you are new to downloading, I recommend using a floppy disk first—but check the size of the file you want to download before starting. You will need to know if it will fit on a floppy disk or if you would like to download directly to your hard drive. If you are planning to download files and programs to your hard drive, it might help to organize your data by making file folders before you download (see the following Tip).

Tip

To make a file folder for downloading, go to:

Start>Programs>Windows Explorer

Find your C Drive and highlight it. Now click File, New, and then Folder. A new folder will appear and you will have to name it. You might label it "Genealogy" or "Family History." When you download a file or program, remember to save it to the folder you just created.

7. If you get ready to open the folder and notice that the folder is blank, check to see whether all of the files are being displayed. The way you do this is to click on the down arrow by Files of Type. Select All Files (see Figure 1.5). By doing this, you can see everything in the file. When you find your downloaded file, double-click on it to open it.

F i g u r e   1 . 5

Dialog box showing All Files.

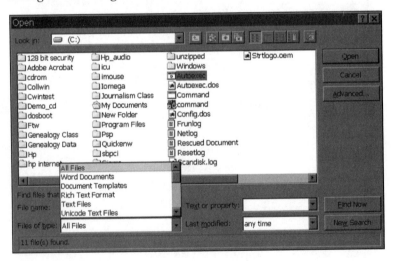

Now you are ready to move to Step 2.

Step 2

Using Web Browsers and Search Engines

Learn to make effective use of your Web browser and Internet Web directories with search engines.

If you already know how to use both of these, proceed to Step 3. Otherwise, follow these procedures.

Know Your Web Browser

You might already have a working knowledge of your computer, but are you familiar with your Web browser? If you do not know what a Web browser is or what Web browser is installed on your computer, the mystery will unravel as you proceed with this step.

Just what is a Web browser? A *Web browser* is software that allows you to view the Internet and move around in it. Many Web browsers are available to Internet users, but the two most popular are Netscape Navigator and Internet Explorer. You might have heard their names without knowing quite what they do. What follows is a brief, easy-to-follow overview of how to use a Web browser to explore the Internet.

Figure 2.1a
The Netscape icon.

Figure 2.1b
The Internet Explorer icon.

Let's begin. Assuming that you have the Internet already installed on your computer, you should see an Internet icon on your computer screen. Just double-click on this icon, and the browser that is already installed on your computer will come up. The first page you see is the *start page*. As soon as you see it, you are "on the 'Net." Once you see the start page, you can start exploring the Internet. If you know of a Web site that you would like to visit, you will need its Internet address, or URL (Universal Resource Locator). Most Internet addresses begin with **http://**, followed by **www.**, a name or descriptive phrase, and an extension such as **.net** or **.com**. An Internet address looks something like this: **http://www.genforum.com**. What does it all mean? Here's the breakdown.

The first part of the URL, before the two slashes, tells the user what method of access is being used at that Web address. The most common prefix to most addresses is **http://**, which is the abbreviation for HyperText Transfer Protocol.

As most people already know, the next part of the address, **www**, stands for World Wide Web. Following **www.**, in our example, is **genforum**, the name or identity of the Web site.

!

Caution

Check the Web address (URL) for errors! It is so easy to slip in a typo when you are entering an Internet address. Some common errors include typing the letter l instead of the number 1, or the letter O instead of a zero. The Internet is not like the postal service, which will often get our mail to its proper destination even if we get a digit wrong in a street number or forget to put on a zip code. Internet addresses are read by computers, not human beings, and computers do only—and exactly—what they are programmed to do. You will not end up at the Web page you want unless you type the *exact* Web address, so *always* double-check.

The last part of the address, the "dot com" we hear about so often, identifies the host of the Web site, letting you know whether the site is maintained by a commercial organization (as in our example), an educational institution, a branch of government or a nonprofit group, among many other possibilities.

Thus the full Internet address for the genealogical resource called GenForum is **http://www.genforum.com**.

As you travel through the World Wide Web, pay close attention to hosts. Generally speaking, government and organization Web sites post information from their official records. You will be seeking credible information, and most of the information posted at government Web sites is documented, allowing you to validate your findings. Here are some host identifiers:

- ◆ **org**—organization (usually nonprofit)
- ◆ **net**—network
- ◆ **mil**—military group or office
- ◆ **gov**—government branch or office
- ◆ **edu**—educational institution
- ◆ **com**—commercial organization

To go to a Web address, you have a couple of options.

Netscape Navigator users can click on the File menu, then on Open Location.

Figure 2.2a

Finding a Web site using Netscape Navigator.

Internet Explorer users can click on the File menu, and then Open.

F i g u r e   2 . 2 b

Finding a Web site using Internet Explorer.

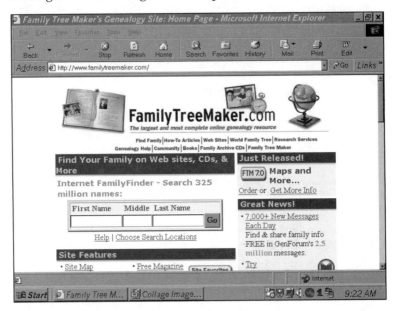

Users of either type of browser can type the Web address (URL) into the address/location box on the browser and then click the Go button.

Now let's look at the functions of your Web browser. The labels on the toolbar buttons for Internet Explorer and Netscape Navigator will vary, but both programs perform the same basic functions.

Go to a Web site and start at the top of your screen (See Figure 2.3.):

Figure 2.3

The Internet Explorer browser screen.

♦ **Title bar**. The colored bar across the very top of your screen will give the name (and possibly a short description) of the Web site you have entered. At the end of that colored bar are the keys for reducing, minimizing and closing the screen.

To close a window, *click on the X* in the top right corner.

To reduce/minimize either a window or the taskbar at the bottom of your screen, *click on the minus sign*.

To reduce the size of the window, while keeping it open and in view, *click on the overlapping squares* located between the X and the minus sign.

♦ **Menu bar**. This bar lists things like File, Edit, View, Favorites, Tools, and Help.

◆ **Tool bar**. This has buttons like the following: Back, Forward, Stop, Reload/Refresh, Home, Search, Favorites, History, Mail, and Print. These functions are described below:

Back—This will take you back to the preceding Web page, the one you viewed last.

Forward—This one moves you to the next Web page.

Stop—This button tells your browser to stop whatever it is doing (like trying to capture and load a page). This function is handy if your computer gets hung up trying to access the data you have asked for.

Reload/Refresh—This reposts the current page. If the page includes a lot of graphics, and the graphics or some of the text fail to come up, clicking the Stop button and then the Reload or Refresh button will probably bring the whole page up.

Home—Any time you are surfing the Web and want to go back to the start page, just hit Home and it will take you there.

Search—Clicking on this button will bring up a list of search engines. Click on the one you want to use.

Bookmarks/Favorites—Favorites (called Bookmarks in Netscape Navigator) provide shortcuts to the pages you visit most often. When you are on a Web page you may want to return to, just click on the button titled Bookmark or Favorites and follow the directions. Remember, though, if you're using a public-access computer, you can't rely on anything being there the next time you use it. The staff usually clears out things like bookmarks on a regular basis.

History—Clicking on this button will display a list of recently visited Web sites.

Print—This button sends a copy of the open page on your browser to the printer. It will print the page exactly as shown. If you want more options, click File, then Print, and then follow directions.

◆ **Address/Location bar**. This displays the address (URL) of the page you are on. You can type another Web address into this bar and click "Go" or "Enter" to go to a new Web site. In Internet Explorer, the bar is known as your Address bar. In Netscape Navigator, the bar is known as your Location bar.

◆ **Window**. The next part of your Web browser is the screen, which has scroll bars on the right side of it. The scroll bars are the thin gray lines at the side of the page that have arrows at the top and bottom. When you click the arrows, the screen moves up and down. Some Web sites also have scroll bars along the bottom of the page to move from side to side.

◆ **Task bar**. This shows which task functions, or windows, are available to open with a click at any given time. You can simultaneously open multiple windows of your Web browser, if you so desire, and work between two tasks or in multiple programs. Working between two or more tasks is called *multitasking*.

Tip

Don't give up too easily if a Web site fails to open or you have trouble making the connection. Here are some hints to help you break through that wall. If a Web site doesn't open, try at least three more times before attempting something else. Web sites get busy, and occasionally it's just difficult to get through all of the traffic. You've heard the saying "third time's a charm." Sometimes it works with Web sites. If it doesn't, try this:

Web addresses (URLs) are broken into sections. For example:

http://www.cyndislist.com/books.htm

From this Web address, we can tell a few things. We already know that **http://www** is the standard preface to most URLs. Likewise, we know that **cyndislist** is the name or description of the Web site's owner, in this case, Cyndi's List. The **.com** tells us that this is a commercial group. But what about the word "**books**"? It tells us we are in the Books section of Cyndi's List. If the Web link is broken, or the address has been changed so that we cannot access the Web site, we can remove this part of the address—or anything that follows the last slash (/). If there are several slashes (/), we can keep removing the letters that follow them until we have pared down to the basic URL, which might connect us to the Web site we are seeking.

In the example above, if we remove **books.htm**, we will be at the home page for Cyndi's List. Experiment with this technique at other Web sites.

SECTION TWO:

Learn About
Web Directories
and Search Engines

Everyone asks, "Where do I begin?" After speaking with many first-time family tree researchers, I have found that everyone's search usually begins in much the same way. Usually, a researcher's first inclination is to use a search engine like Yahoo! and type in the individual name or family name that they are researching.

If you haven't tried this yet, just go to Yahoo! and type in your family's surname. Your search might yield hundreds, maybe even thousands, of Web pages with your family's surname on them—but very few will have any genealogical data. If you have an unusual or rare name, you may find only a few pages with your family name on them, but these also will give you little, if any, information about your genealogy. Occasionally, people do find part of their family tree this way, but it's not very likely.

That's why I'm devoting a whole section to Web directories and search engines. To understand why a search engine like Yahoo! won't usually give you the genealogy you're looking for, you also have to understand how Web directories work and how to make them work for you.

What is a Web Directory?

A *Web directory* functions like a phone directory. The white pages list residential phone numbers, and some businesses, alphabetically and by town. The Yellow Pages categorizes and alphabetizes services, organizations, businesses, physicians—everything from Automobile Dealers to Zoos. Without a logical system, we would never find a phone number.

The Internet works the same way. There are hundreds of Web directories out there in cyberspace. Among the more popular ones—those you might have heard of in addition to Yahoo!—are AltaVista, Lycos, MSN, HotBot, and Web Crawler. In the early days of the Internet, its primary users were the military, libraries, universities, and government entities. These groups categorized things to suit them. When the general public wanted to use the Internet, as we now know it, there was really no consistent, orderly system for doing so. So attempts were made to catalog the Web in a way that anyone could understand. Each Web directory now organizes Web pages into categories. You can look through each of the directory's categories or you can use its search engine.

What is a Search Engine?

A *search engine* is nothing more than a computer program that looks through categories of online information (like flipping through the Yellow Pages) until it finds what you are seeking. It posts results immediately. Most Web directories have some type of search engine.

Several factors distinguish Web directories and their search engines from one another, but the main one is the way they catalog and file each Web page within a Web site. Some search engines are programmed to search only the title (and a brief description) of each Web page they locate. Others look for keywords in the titles and also search for the keyword in the body of every page. If you performed the same keyword search on each Web directory, your results would vary considerably, and so would the number of actual matches.

There are hundreds of search engines on the Internet. Deciding which one to use is impossible without experimenting with several, because no single Web directory has categorized the entire World Wide Web. If you are conducting a serious search, visit different search engines to find one or two that deliver more of the particular kind of information you want. Here is a short list of some of the more prominent search engines. AltaVista is at the top because it is currently the biggest search engine on the Internet.

AltaVista	**http://www.altavista.com**
Excite	**http://www.excite.com**
Yahoo!	**http://www.yahoo.com**
Infoseek	**http://www.infoseek.go.com**
Go To	**http://www.goto.com**
Lycos	**http://www.lycos.com**
HotBot	**http://www.hotbot.com**
Microsoft Network Search	**http://search.msn.com**
Web Crawler	**http://www.webcrawler.com**
Dogpile	**http://www.dogpile.com**
Magellan	**http://magellan.excite.com**

Some Web sites will give you search results from multiple search engines at once. In my opinion, the best one of these is Ask Jeeves at **http://www.ask.com** (see Figure 2.4). New Internet surfers will appreciate how easy it is to use. Jeeves lets you search by actually asking a question. Just type in your question and Jeeves will retrieve up to ten answers from five separate search engines. Jeeves also keeps previously asked questions in its "memory," so if you ask the same question more than once, it will instantly post the answer. Ah, technology!

F i g u r e   2 . 4

The Ask Jeeves site.

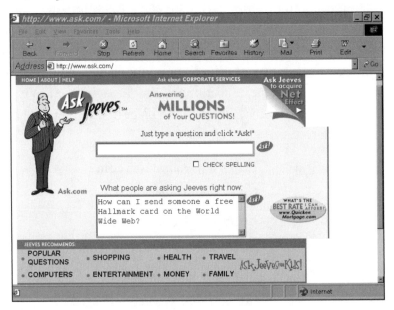

Much of your research will focus on your distant ancestors. If you are searching for living relatives, though, try:

WHOWHERE PEOPLE FINDER (by Lycos)

http://www.whowhere.lycos.com

Figure 2.5

The WhoWhere People Finder site. Bigfoot is another great search site for locating living individuals.

BIGFOOT

http://www.bigfoot.com

Figure 2.6

The Bigfoot site.

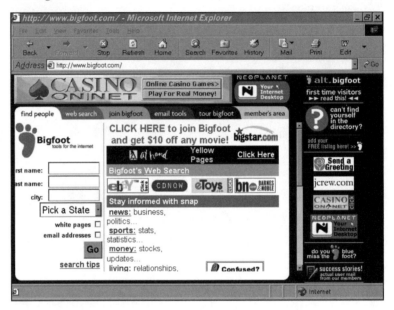

Many people will tell you searching the Web is easy, but don't be misled. Anyone, including my children, can go to a search engine and type in a word, but the returns they get will depend, most importantly, on the search engine that they used. So, let's discuss how to get the most out of a Web directory. Using the Magellan Internet Guide as our example, go to Magellan's Web site at **http://magellan.excite.com,** and you will immediately notice the many categories of information it indexes.

F i g u r e   2 . 7

Magellan Internet Guide home page.

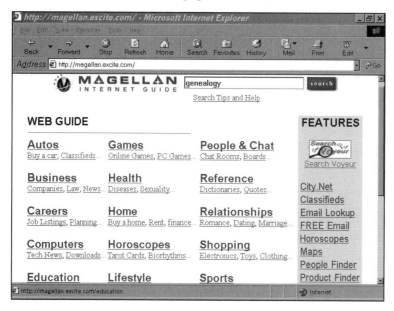

To find the topic "Genealogy," click on the following hyperlinks in this order:

Lifestyle > Hobbies/Interests > Genealogy

You can see from this layout just how the Web directory is categorized. From the home page, each topic has a heading like Auto, Business, and Careers. Under each heading will be subtopics. Under the heading *Auto*, notice the subtopics *Buy a Car* and *Classifieds*. Each category will contain hundreds, maybe thousands, of links to other Web sites. Not every Web directory is organized in a manner that lets you see all of the links like this. Some Web directories, like AltaVista, do file the same information and links in multiple categories. For instance, at AltaVista, you will find Genealogy & Heraldry not only under Home & Family, but also under Hobbies & Interests.

Many Web directories are popular because of their "cool" name or the fact that they have been around so long. But the bottom line is how much data you can find and how good it is. I like to use a highly underrated Web site called About.com (formerly known as The Mining Company). Its slogan says: "We mine the net so you don't have to."

About.com is different from most other Web directories. Real people, or "guides," make About.com a joy to use. These forum moderators and Webmasters are qualified to maintain their area of interest on the Web site. They live and work in the fields of interest they oversee. Visitors to the site can e-mail the guides and make requests for coverage of specific topics. The guides are actively involved in the site content. The site is set up in a consistent, user-friendly format in each section. To understand how About.com works, let's explore. Go to About.com's Web site (see Figure 2.8) at **http://www.about.com**.

Figure 2.8

The About.com home page.

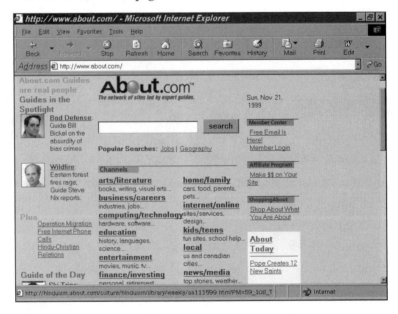

To access the genealogy area of this Web site, connect through the following links:

> Hobbies > Pastimes > Genealogy

From the genealogy page, the first thing you will notice is an introduction to your site guide. Then you will see a "You are here" template that reviews the links that brought you to this page (see Figure 2.9).

Figure 2.9

The About.com genealogy page.

On each of About.com's topic Web sites you will find links under Content, TalkAbout, and ShopAbout. At About.com's genealogy section, under TalkAbout, you have the chance to post to community bulletin boards, chat, and communicate with other researchers. The articles at this site are informative and intelligently written, just as they are in About.com's other Web page categories. Don't put off checking out this unique Web community.

> *"A family history shows*
> *that you have lived."*
>
> —Anonymous quote from the Internet

Now you are ready to move to Step 3.

Step 3

Jumping onto the 'Net!

Okay, this is the *big* step you've been working toward. If you have done everything in Steps 1 and 2, your ancestor search will be much easier and more enjoyable.

SECTION ONE:
The Vast World
of Cyberspace

I've listed several Web sites in this section, with a brief overview of each. I have also noted which Web sites have a searchable database—a type of index that allows users to find specific names or other pieces of identifying information among the massive amounts of data stored on the Web site. A searchable database for a given Web site has a search engine, but one that works only at that site.

Now, let's get started. Our first stop will be the Web site that I consider the best of all online genealogical resources: Cyndi's List of Genealogy Sites on the Internet. Cyndi Howells, who created this Web site, has been a genealogist for more than nineteen years. She is the Webmaster for the Tacoma-Pierce County Genealogical Society in Washington. For Cyndi, what started as a project for her local genealogy society turned into one of the most extensive resources for genealogy research on the Internet today. Cyndi is the sole owner of Cyndi's List. At this writing, the Web site has more than 50,000 links, cross-referenced into one hundred different categories. It has no searchable database, but it provides an index to the huge array of other genealogy sites on the Internet. As you become familiar with the Internet's genealogy communities, you will return to Cyndi's List many, many times. On your first visit, plan to spend twenty or thirty minutes looking through this vast collection. You will be amazed to see what is waiting for you out there in cyberspace.

CYNDI'S LIST

http://www.cyndislist.com

Figure 3.1

The Cyndi's List home page.

This is the best of the best, the cream of the crop, the top dog of all Web sites for genealogy research. This should be everyone's first stop in the search for family roots and history. Cyndi's List is huge. It is exciting to see everything Cyndi has pulled together and categorized, but the challenge is to learn how to find what you need amid the abundance. Cyndi's List is like the Super Wal-Mart of genealogy on the Internet. Have you ever tried to find one small item, like a bottle of shampoo, in one of these large retail chain stores? It could be on the supermarket side under toiletries or on the retail side in cosmetics. You know it's somewhere in the acres of aisles, but you don't know where to look. As with everything, practice makes perfect! The more often you go to Wal-Mart, the better you know its layout. The more often you surf the genealogy Web sites, the more familiar you will become with their locations, their information, and the way they organize them.

Searching for one name on the Internet can be like looking for a needle in a haystack. There are thousands of genealogy Web sites on the Internet and millions of names in their databases. What if you were looking for someone in your family named Thomas Melton, who lived in Martin County, Indiana, in the early part of the 1800s? You probably should not begin with a major database that lists millions of names, because searching for a common name like Thomas Melton could bring you hundreds of returns. Then you could spend hours sifting through the names and trying to figure out which could belong to your relative. Since you know where he lived and approximately when he lived there, your best bet would be a smaller, regional database like U.S. GenWeb. Regional database searches provide a good launching pad for your research.

THE GENWEB PROJECT
AND THE U.S. GENWEB PROJECT

http://www.worldgenweb.org and

http://www.usgenweb.org
   *searchable database**

F i g u r e   3 . 2
The U.S. GenWeb Project home page.

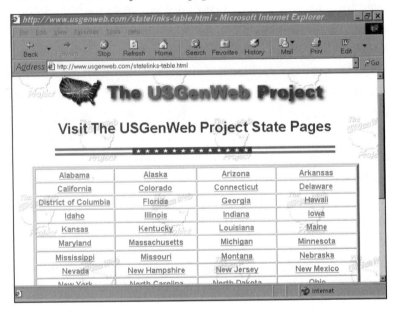

This is one fantastic site! It will let you access and even exchange information that you would have a hard time finding elsewhere. GenWeb's world site is divided into fifteen world regions, which in turn are divided by countries. Each country divides further into individual provinces, states, or counties. The site also maintains a free online digital library through the World GenWeb Project Archives.

The U.S. GenWeb Project makes searching within the U.S. almost effortless, because information is indexed at the state, county, and even township or city levels. What makes this project unique, however, is its volunteers who gather, record, and publish the information to the Internet GenWeb site for their area.

The volunteers for some counties have pulled together remarkable information. You might be surprised to find diaries, biographies, census records, military records, city and county histories, family histories, vital records for births, deaths and marriages, church records, family Bibles, wills, deeds, tombstone inscriptions, and more. Occasionally, you will find only minimal information. This is usually because researchers in that area are still gathering and organizing data, so check back often. A few counties in each state post a little sign saying, "Adopt me." In these cases, U.S. GenWeb is still looking for volunteers to sponsor those counties.

Most of the county sites in U.S. GenWeb will let you post a query. This is a great place to make contact with other people who might be researching some of the same people you are, since, at the county level, you are more likely to find information specific to your family.

You might also, through exchanges of information with other researchers, come across materials that would help with the GenWeb effort. In this case, contact the U.S. GenWeb sponsor listed for the area for which you have data. Much of what you find on GenWeb for your own research will have been posted by a volunteer.

Sites that are larger and more comprehensive than GenWeb are great resources when you have exhausted other outlets or when you are researching an unusual name. Most large Web sites offer great tips for using their search engines. Take heed! Since the databases are so huge—usually with millions of names—you might want to start your search by filling in all of the research data that they request.

If your search turns up nothing, or only a few returns that don't match what you need, try a different search. This time, remove some information, such as a birth date or death date. Still no results? Try removing all of the data except the name. If all else fails, enter *only* a surname. This has worked for me. These databases include the names of other researchers like you, who have submitted their family trees to be published on the Internet. If the submitter has one of your relatives in his or her tree *by name only*, without any birth date or other information, your database search will take you to that source if you, too, have entered only the name, eliminating dates and other facts. When you use large databases at sites like Family Tree Maker, follow their tips for searching. The method by which you search will depend upon how each Web site indexes its records.

FAMILY TREE MAKER

http://www.familytreemaker.com

searchable database

F i g u r e   3 . 3

The Family Tree Maker home page.

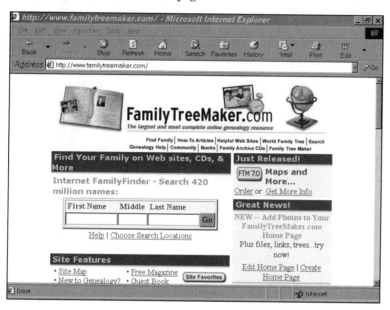

The Family Tree Maker (FTM) Web site is phenomenal for accessing family trees, biographies, and military records. From FTM's home page, you will see the Internet Family Finder (IFF). Just below the IFF, click on the link that says "Choose search locations." You will be taken to the Internet Family Finder search engine, with options that will allow you to perform a selective search. *Now* type a name that you are searching for in the boxes provided. Here's the key to a productive search, which will display only results that you can access immediately online:

Make sure that the *only* boxes you check below the name you have entered are the ones that offer to search the Internet and User Home Pages, Message Boards, Classifieds, Civil War Databases, and Family Tree Maker Online. This is the only way you can search FTM and gather the information you need for free. You can choose to search *all* of the categories listed, but that could carry a fee; for a free search, use the method I have just described.

If you do check all possible boxes, the search engine will look through FTM's collection of compact discs and the Genealogy Library online for matches. If your search produces a match that says, for example, CD #7, FTM will take you to an advertisement for their compact discs. They have a monumental collection of CDs containing family trees and archived indexes to records worldwide. The cost for FTM's compact discs varies depending on whether you purchase one CD or a price-discounted bundle. FTM does a lot of special pricing and offers bundles of CDs at an average of only about $8 to $10 per CD. I have used the CDs, and they contain a wealth of information. I know of one genealogy library in my home area that has its own collection of FTM's CDs. I'm sure many other genealogy libraries and historical societies purchase them with patrons' donations.

Family Tree Maker also offers free genealogy home pages, message boards, and genealogy classifieds. GenealogyLibrary.com, as mentioned previously, is FTM's attempt to create a massive genealogy library by publishing individual family history books online. GenealogyLibrary.com is a fast-growing collection of more than 2,000 databases. The site, on average, uploads three new books per day. The search engine at this site gives you the convenience of searching by category, individual book or the entire online library for ancestors or family histories. Here you will find hundreds of rare, hard-to-find books, right at your fingertips. The subscription cost for this service is reasonable.

Sometime in the future, you will probably want to submit your family tree to FTM for its World Family Tree (WFT). To do so, you will first need to put your information into GEDCOM format, which allows family trees to be transferred from one computer to another, regardless of the family tree software being used. Publishing your family tree on the Internet will help it grow and will put you in touch with other researchers, with whom you can exchange data and tips. This is definitely one of the easiest ways to broaden your research and knowledge.

FAMILY SEARCH

http://www.familysearch.org
searchable database

Figure 3.4

The Family Search home page.

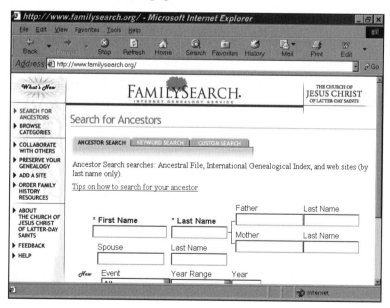

Family Search is the newest genealogy Web site online, opened by the Church of Jesus Christ of Latter-day Saints, also known as the Mormon Church, in the spring of 1999. The church began by placing about 400 *million* names of deceased individuals in an online free-access database. Some entries are in family files, others are recorded individually. The first week the Web site was up and running, it received millions of visits, called *hits* in Web talk. Immediately, more computer servers were brought in to handle the number of people trying to visit the Web site. The first time I tried to use the site that week, I had a one-and-a-half hour wait to get in; then I was allowed only half an hour to use the database. Despite the long wait and short access, I hit pay dirt the first time. The frenzy has since let up, so you can gain immediate access.

The number of records at this site is astounding. The Web site's database is part of the world's largest genealogical repository, the Family History Library™ in downtown Salt Lake City, Utah. This enormous archive is a result of the church's century-old commitment to gathering family records worldwide. The Web site's features include Search for Ancestors, Collaborate (with other researchers), and Preserve Genealogy (by submitting your family tree). Searches from this Web site will produce matches from the International Genealogical Index (IGI) and Ancestral Files. The IGI lists millions of names of deceased persons throughout the world. Names in the IGI records come from vital records from the early 1500s to 1885, and many others have been submitted by members of the Church of Jesus Christ of Latter-day Saints. Matches found in the IGI are linked to the Family History Library catalog, giving the researcher source information. Ancestral Files are simply that—files of ancestors that have been submitted to the Family History Library by church members and the general public. The Ancestral Files link families into pedigrees showing ancestors and descendants. This is the single largest Web site for genealogy records, and it is still growing! If you're wondering about the cost for all of this—it's *free*.

ANCESTRY

http://www.ancestry.com

searchable database

Figure 3.5

The Ancestry site.

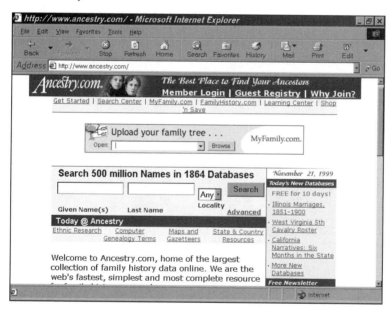

This Web site contains the Ancestry World Tree, Ancestry's equivalent of FTM's World Family Tree. As with FTM's program, you can submit your family tree in a computer format known as GEDCOM. The Web site will tell you how to do this. At this writing, Ancestry is offering free access to the Ancestry World Tree, Social Security Index, and some of its new databases. Every day, Ancestry adds new databases, allowing everyone free access to them for the first ten days. After the ten-day free period, the database is archived, and you must become an Ancestry subscriber to search the archived databases and view their contents. Accessing Ancestry's many other databases requires membership, which can be purchased annually or quarterly. A few other databases housed at this site are the Periodical Source Index Articles, Biographies, Vital Records, and Military Records. Ancestry is a great database of literature and considers itself an online genealogy library of sorts. Ancestry is, in my opinion, one of the most user-friendly Web sites for genealogy research on the Internet today.

ROOTSWEB

http://www.rootsweb.com
searchable database

F i g u r e   3 . 6

The RootsWeb home page.

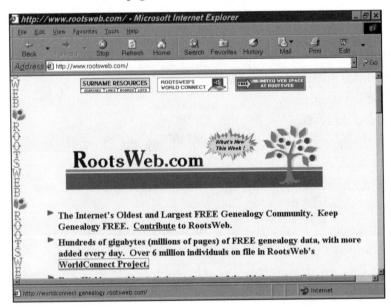

RootsWeb, founded in 1987, is the Internet's oldest and largest genealogy community. Its search engines are set up to scour the Social Security Death Index, census extracts, county history indices, and home pages. Information at RootsWeb can be accessed for free; however, a contribution is always appreciated. If you choose to become a member of RootsWeb, annual memberships start at $12. You will want to read everything this site suggests about using and accessing the information there. RootsWeb's biggest contribution to the genealogy community is probably the sheer number of researchers who have been brought together since the Web site was launched. RootsWeb also works hand in hand with the very popular GenWeb, and together they are a great resource for any genealogist!

Let's take a closer look at RootsWeb. ROOTS-L, the original mailing list for the genealogy community, was founded in 1987 and is still going strong, with more than 10,000 subscribers. ROOTS-L is a very broad-based mailing list, covering all aspects of genealogy. Over the years, many volunteers have started and maintained separate database projects in cooperation with RootsWeb participants. The RootsWeb Surname List is one of those projects. Founded in 1988, it is a registry of more than 600,000 surnames compiled by more than 75,000 researchers. The list continues to grow, with more than 700 surnames being added daily. If you have already done any family history research on the Internet, you have no doubt stumbled across this outstanding Web site. Like many people, though, you might not have known how to put it to its best use.

Beginning at RootsWeb's home page, let's look halfway down the page, on the left-hand side, under Genealogy Community. There you will see a number of links listed under Search Engines. Start with searching the RSL, since that is listed first. From the RSL search page, type in a *surname only,* because this search engine is not designed to look for individuals. After typing in the surname and searching, your result might look something like this:

F i g u r e   3 . 7

An example of a RootsWeb search result.

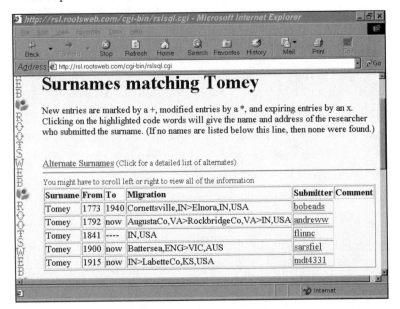

Here is how to read the information above:

1. The first column is, of course, the surname for which you searched.

2. The second column is the earliest date for which the submitter (the author of the information) has records for that surname.

3. The third column is the most recent date for which the submitter has records for that surname.

4. The fourth column shows the migration of the submitter's family. An arrow (>) between state or country abbreviation shows the record of movement between regions.

5. The fifth column is the name by which RootsWeb identifies the submitter. This ID name will be underlined. Just click on it, and it will take you to a page where you will find the name, postal address, and/or e-mail address of the researcher who has submitted the information on that family name.

> *"There is no king who has not had a slave among his ancestors, and no slave who has not had a king among his."*
>
> —Helen Keller

RootsWeb has mailing lists for individual surnames. If I want to search for information on Thomas Melton, I simply search through the Melton Family Mailing List. This mailing list is composed of people like myself who are searching and sharing information about the Melton surname. Although we may not all be searching within the same lineage, we can share information that we have gathered from other sources, even if it doesn't fit into our own family record. For instance, if I gathered information from a courthouse, but it didn't pertain to my tree, I might still post it to the Internet to give another Melton researcher the chance to make a connection.

GENCONNECT

http://cgi.rootsweb.com/~genbbs

Figure 3.8

GenConnect at RootsWeb.

This is yet another extension of the RootsWeb Project. It started as a query board for a single Kentucky GenWeb county page, but it grew rapidly into a worldwide project, placing query boards on county and state levels within GenWeb. In April 1998, GenConnect emerged in its current form. Since then, GenConnect has been upgraded several times, each time with exciting new features. Currently, GenConnect offers a suite of seven boards: Bibles, Biographies, Deeds, Obituaries, Queries, Pensions, and Wills.

GENEALOGY PORTAL.COM

http://www.genealogyportal.com

searchable database

Figure 3.9

GenealogyPortal.com.

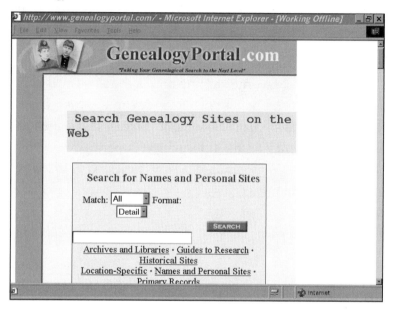

Genealogy Portal.com is a joint effort by Matt Helm (Helm's Genealogy Toolbox) and Steve Wood (The Genealogy Home Page). Genealogy Portal.com has been created to help genealogists locate information that is not readily accessible through traditional genealogy links and sites. The site features eight separate search engines that sort through a variety of genealogy information online. The titles of the eight search engines are Archives and Libraries, Names and Personal Sites, Guides to Research, Primary Records, Historical Sites, Research Supplies, Location-Specific, and Software and Utilities.

Steve Wood's Genealogy Home Page, at http://www.genhomepage.com, is one of the oldest genealogy Web sites on the Internet. It is a massive Web site with more than fifteen categories for searching. Matt Helm and his wife, April, manage Helm's Genealogy Toolbox. The Toolbox is much like Cyndi's List. It is divided into seven areas of genealogy research, containing a total of more than 70,000 links to the Toolbox. Access the Tool box at **http://www.genealogytoolbox.com**.

This is my list of favorite starting points. I hope it will help you discover where and how to begin your search. From these sites, you can tap into so many others out there. It's now time to begin your journey on the Information Superhighway. You will be astounded at what you find. Many dedicated volunteers have made this journey possible. Be sure to thank them along the way!

Connecting the Links

Let's have a quick review here. In the last section, we covered seven of the very best genealogy Web sites the Internet has to offer.

- ◆ Cyndi's List
  http://www.cyndislist.com
- ◆ The U.S. GenWeb Project
  http://www.usgenweb.org
- ◆ Family Tree Maker
  http://www.familytreemaker.com
- ◆ Family Search
  http://www.familysearch.org
- ◆ Ancestry
  http://www.ancestry.com
- ◆ RootsWeb
  http://www.rootsweb.com
- ◆ Genealogy Portal.com
  http://www.genealogyportal.com

In Section One, we explored some of the most comprehensive genealogy Web sites in cyberspace, but even these are only the tip of the iceberg. Let's take a look at some other Web sites that can speed you on your journey.

Tip

Bookmark Web sites that pertain to your family search. If you are not accustomed to bookmarking, start practicing now. Internet Explorer calls these placeholders "Favorites," and Netscape Navigator calls them "Bookmarks." You can find them in either browser by clicking on the toolbar.

To make your Web browser user-friendly, set up your bookmarks in folders, using a different folder for each surname that you are working on.

To set up a folder in Internet Explorer, click Favorites, then click Organize Favorites. Click on Create Folder and give your folder a name. To set up a folder in Netscape Navigator, the process is similar. Click on Bookmarks, then Edit Bookmarks. To create a new folder, just highlight the top folder, then right-click on your mouse and select New Folder and give it a name. When you find a Web site that contains genealogy information that you want to save, bookmark it. Then click and drag the Bookmark or Favorite to a folder that you have created in your Internet program. I find it useful to make individual folders for genealogy and for each surname I am researching.

Searchable Databases

GENTREE

http://www.gentree.com

Figure 3.10

GenTree Home Page

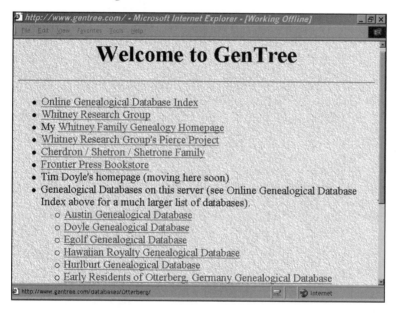

GenTree, the Online Genealogical Database Index, contains links to all known genealogical databases searchable through the Web. It is limited to searchable databases and does *not* include links to sites devoted to specific families unless they have databases available for searching. This site takes you directly to the Web sites of family databases online.

To enter and use GenTree:

1. Go to the GenTree Home Page at **http://www.gentree.com**.

2. The first link on the page says Online Genealogical Database Index. Click here.

3. Go down the page to "Access The Index." Click on the initial letter of the surname you are searching for.

4. Look through the results until you see the surname. If you find it, click on the link and view the entire file of names to see if your family is connected in any way to the family files on display.

5. If you reach a Web page with information that matches anything in your family tree, you will want to contact the person who published the information. You can usually go to the bottom of the Web page and look for submitter information or maybe a link that says Home. This will take you to the home page of the person who put the family tree on the Internet. This is a great way to make contact with other people researching branches of your family tree.

SURNAMEWEB

http://www.surnameweb.org

Figure 3.11

The Surname Web site.

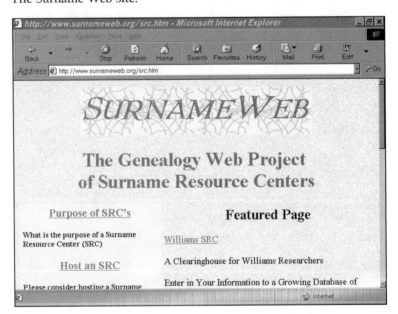

This searches for surnames anywhere on the Internet and brings them to a central location, providing origins, Web page links, home pages, resource centers, and a patented search system. SurnameWeb is developing a sister site that will provide the simplest of access to non-surname genealogy sites and genealogy data on the Web. There are four components to the SurnameWeb site: Surname Registry, Surname Resource Center, Other Surname Resources and Databases, and Home Page Construction Kit.

From SurnameWeb:

> "One thing we have discovered is that we are a nation of wanderers. Our ancestors have wandered the globe, and often left us with only one clue to trace their heritage, their surname. Because of this, we suggest that we establish Surname Resource Centers, where all the information available on a surname can be centrally located. Dennis Partridge has set up The Partridge Nest, a place for all Partridge's and the variant spellings of that surname. What we propose is that you build a nest for one of your major surnames too, someplace where you can gather all your cousins together. The SurnameWeb links to all the nests on the Web—there are more than 2,100 so far—where you can go to meet your cousins."

SURNAME SPRINGBOARD

http://www.geocities.com/Heartland/2154/spring.htm

Figure 3.12
Surname Springboard.

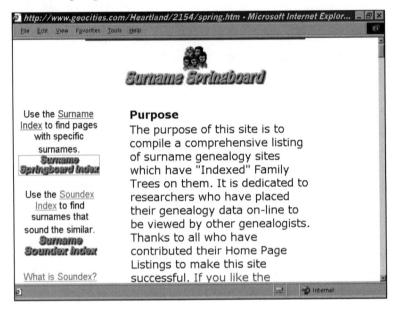

This site does the same thing as SurnameWeb. Its purpose is to compile a comprehensive listing of surname genealogy sites that have "indexed" family trees on them. Surname Springboard was started by Karen Basile of Karen's Genealogy Sources (**http://www.toltbbs.com/~kbasile**). The site was previously maintained by Steve Lacy, owner of Genealogy Gateway™ To The Web. On May 17, 1997, Allen Lacy, of Allen Lacy's Genealogy Page (**http://www.allenlacy.com/index.html**), took over the Surname Springboard. As of this writing, Surname Springboard has forty-seven pages, with a maximum of fifty links per page. Each page contains information on more than 12,000 surnames. For easy access to the surnames, you can take advantage of the alphabetical Surname Index. The Index is hyperlinked to these pages for quick access to each surname. There also is a Soundex Index where you can locate surnames that are closely related. Go to the home page, click on "Surname Springboards Index," and follow the letters until you find whether the surname for which you are searching is listed. If you don't find the surname, use the Surname Soundex Index.

N o t e

The National Archives established The Soundex system as a means of indexing the U.S. census schedules, beginning with the 1880 census. The code groups together surnames that sound the same or similar but are spelled differently.

The advantage of Soundex is its ability to group names by sound rather than the exact spelling. A census taker or a family might spell the same surname various ways, but with the use of Soundex, finding families within census schedules is much easier. The existing indexes for the 1880, 1900, 1910, and 1920 federal census enumerations all use the Soundex code.

The code is always one letter plus three digits. The letter is also the first letter of the surname. If the surname is Melton, for example, the Soundex designation begins with "M."

The digits come from the coding system below. In the example of Melton, the code is M435. If the name were Milton, which sounds similar to Melton, the code is still M435.

> 1 = B,P,F,V
> 2 = C,S,G,J,K,Q,X,Z
> 3 = D,T
> 4 = L
> 5 = M,N
> 6 = R

The letters A,E,I,O,U,Y,H, and W are not coded.

Note that surname prefixes such as van, Von, Di, de, le, D', dela, or du are sometimes disregarded in alphabetizing and in coding.

GENGATEWAY

http://www.gengateway.com/mainsite.htm or

http://www.gengateway.com

F i g u r e   3 . 1 3

Genealogy Gateway

This is probably the largest group of genealogy and history home page services and links on the Internet. With more than 42,000 categorized and alphabetized resource listings, this very popular, award-winning site is growing rapidly. Stop by to browse all the free services and resource offerings. The largest listing of online newspaper obituary searches and Scottish links on the Internet are also found here. This Web site is operated independently by Steve Lacy, who created and developed it.

> *"Only a genealogist regards*
> *a step backwards as progress."*
>
> —Anonymous quote from the Internet

LINEAGES

http://www.lineages.com

Figure 3.14

Lineages Home Page

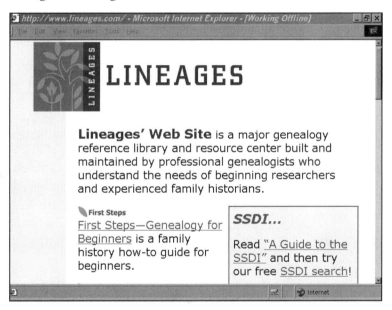

This is a Web site along the same lines as Family Tree Maker and Ancestry. Lineages is a major genealogy reference library and resource center, built and maintained by professional genealogists who understand the needs of beginning researchers and experienced family historians. Lineages was founded in

January 1983 by Johni Cerny, former director of research and member of the board of directors for the Institute of Family Research. This site's ease of use makes searching on the Internet a joy.

At the home page, click on Next of Kin. From there, you can search by surname or Soundex. Once you find a match, you will notice that the information is laid out on-screen in the same family tree style that the Family Search (**www.familysearch.org**) site uses. The files are on the Internet in GEDCOM format. If you find a match, you can order the entire GEDCOM family file for only $4.00. From inception, this Web site's mission has been to produce a wide variety of carefully researched projects that give its clients an accurate and meaningful picture of their family history.

GENSOURCE

http://www.gensource.com

F i g u r e   3 . 1 5

Gensource

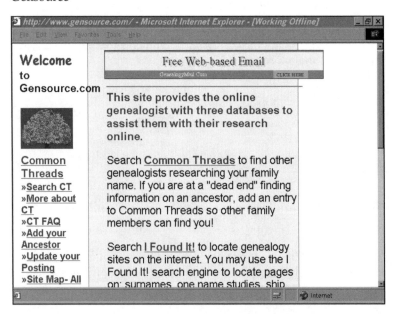

Here are three major databases for online research at one Web site. The three databases are Common Threads, I Found It!, and I Found It! Archives. This is a very user-friendly, detailed Web site that will uncover information not easily found at other genealogy sites.

◆ *Common Threads* puts you in touch with other people who are researching the same family name you are, although not necessarily the same lineage. This database is really helpful if you have reached a dead end in your research, because it contains more than 19,000 unique surnames.

◆ *I Found It!* uses a search engine to comb the Internet for genealogy sites that can assist you in your search. Go to I Found It! and type in a surname. The search engine will locate your surname in personal family histories, church records, census schedules, and more.

◆ *I Found It! Archives* is an index of Web sites that contain actual historical data. The search engine will help you locate an ancestor through transcribed historical records like census schedules and ship lists.

GENEANET GENEALOGICAL DATABASE NETWORK

http://www.geneanet.org

Figure 3.16
The GeneaNet Genealogical Database Network home page.

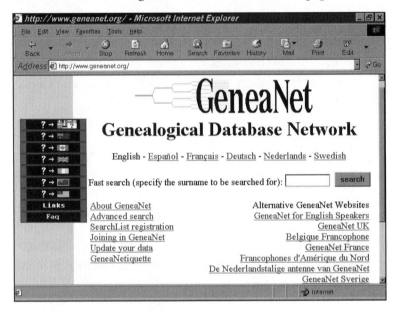

GeneaNet works much the same way that RootsWeb does, and the results look similar. The goal of GeneaNet is to use the power of the Internet to build a database indexing all the genealogical resources over the world, online as well as offline. This site is a good one for finding other researchers looking into the same name or lineage that you are. From the home page, type in your surname in the box at the top of the page. The results will include direct online links to family histories, genealogical publications, manuscripts from libraries and archives, and official sources like church registers and deeds.

The Web sites I've listed in this section will lead you to many, many others that would take too long to mention or discuss here. A large, general site like GenWeb can take you to more specific ones, like regional databases. If, for example, you want to conduct research from Daviess County, Indiana, you can do so by following links from a map of the United States on GenWeb's home page.

In the next section, I list a Web site address where you can find individual states' archives. A few states still do not allow Internet access to state archives, but the majority offer Internet access to census, marriage, divorce, birth, and death records. In the few instances where access to state archives is not available, you will find a listing to a different Web site for each state. This listing will lead you to a state genealogy society or library, where someone online will look up information for you.

Many genealogy Web sites have people who will look things up for a nominal charge or for free. Let us assume you need a birth certificate. In most cases, you can find someone to locate the record and send you a copy of the certificate for a dollar or two. Beginning researchers often find state archives a good place to start.

Some state archives also offer many useful links to additional Web sites with more genealogy and state history. Jump in and see where the links take you. Sometimes the best information is what you find just by wandering the Internet.

Tip

Be sure to make copies of everything you find. Printing Web pages directly off the Internet is a great way to keep track of your research, because each Web site's Internet address is printed at the top or bottom of each page. At a later date, if you need to go back and retrieve or search for more information, you will have the address at your fingertips.

State Archives

ALABAMA

http://alaweb.asc.edu

Alabama State Home Page

F i g u r e   3 . 1 7

AlaWeb; Official Web site for the State of Alabama.

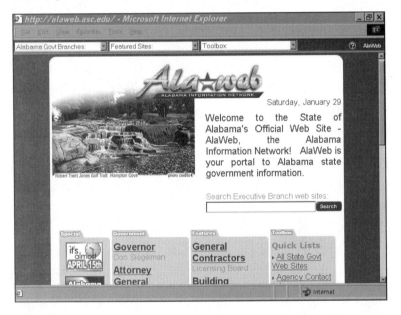

ALASKA

http://www.educ.state.ak.us/lam/library/is/akgene.html

Alaska Genealogy

ARIZONA

http://www.lib.az.us/archives/index.html

Arizona Archives

Figure 3.18

Arizona History & Archives Division.

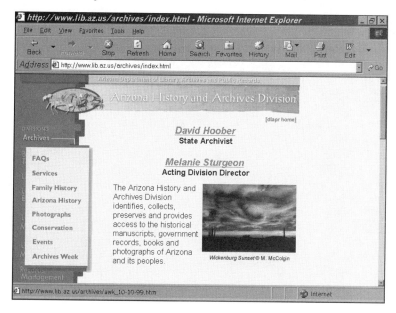

ARKANSAS

http://www.couchgenweb.com/arkansas

The Original Arkansas Genealogy

CALIFORNIA

http://www.ss.ca.gov/archives/archives.htm

California State Archives

F i g u r e   3 . 1 9

California State Archives and Golden State Museum

COLORADO

http://www.state.co.us/gov_dir/gss/archives/index.html

Colorado State Archives

CONNECTICUT

http://www.cslib.org

Connecticut State Library

Figure 3.20

Connecticut State Library

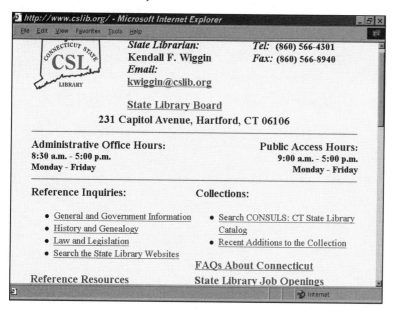

DELAWARE

http://www.lib.de.us/archives

Delaware Public Archives

FLORIDA

http://dlis.dos.state.fl.us/barm/fsa.html

The Florida State Archives

Figure 3.21

The Florida State Archives home page.

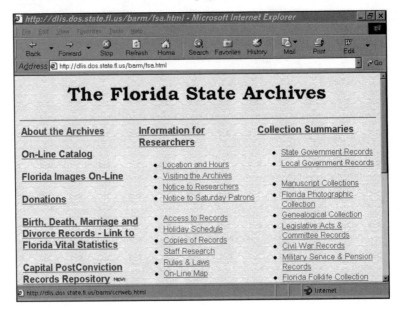

GEORGIA

http://www.sos.state.ga.US/archives

Georgia Department of Archives and History

HAWAII

http://www.state.hi.us/dags/archives/
Hawaii State Archives Home Page

Figure 3.22

Hawaii State Archives Home Page

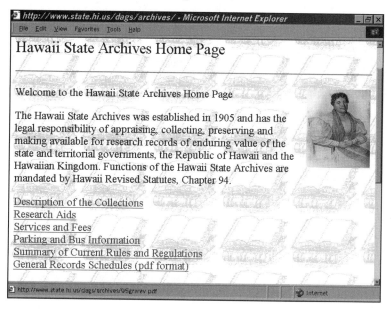

IDAHO

http://www.lib.uidaho.edu/special-collections
Special Collections and Archives of University of Idaho Library

ILLINOIS

http://www.sos.state.il.us/depts/archives/arc_home.html

Illinois Gateway State Archives

F i g u r e   3 . 2 3

Illinois State Archives

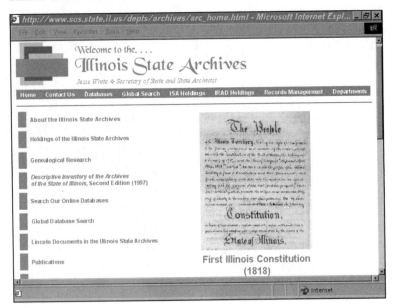

First Illinois Constitution
(1818)

INDIANA

http://www.ai.org/icpr/index.html

Indiana Commission on Public Records

IOWA

http://www.idph.state.ia.us

Iowa Department of Public Health

KANSAS

http://www.kshs.org

Kansas State Historical Society

Figure 3.24

Kansas State Historical Society

KENTUCKY

http://www.kdla.state.ky.us

Kentucky Department for Libraries and Archives

F i g u r e   3 . 2 5

Kentucky Department for Libraries and Archives

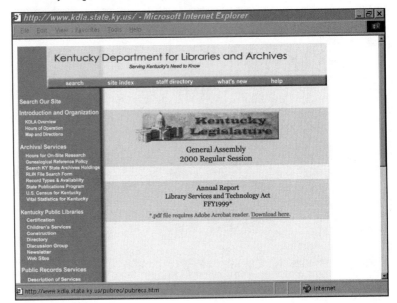

LOUISIANA

http://www.sec.state.la.us/arch-1.htm

Louisiana Archives

Figure 3.26

The Louisiana State Archives

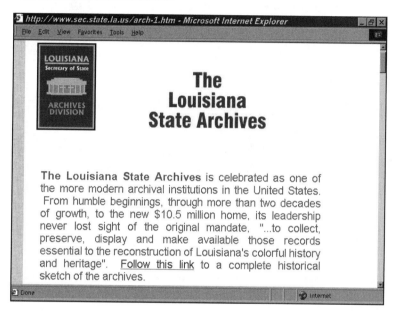

MAINE

http://www.state.me.us/sos/arc/general/admin/mawww001.htm

Maine State Archives

MARYLAND

http://www.mdarchives.state.md.us

Maryland State Archives

MASSACHUSETTS

http://www.magnet.state.ma.us/sec/arc

Massachusetts Archives

MICHIGAN

http://www.sos.state.mi.us/history/archive/archive.html

State Archives of Michigan

F i g u r e   3 . 2 7

State Archives of Michigan

MINNESOTA

http://www.mtn.org/mgs

Minnesota Genealogical Society

MISSISSIPPI

http://www.mdah.state.ms.us

Mississippi Department of Archives and History

Figure 3.28
Mississippi Department of Archives and History

MISSOURI

http://mosl.sos.state.mo.us/rec-man/arch.html

Missouri State Archives

MONTANA

http://www.rootsweb.com/~mtmsgs

Montana Genealogy Society

NEBRASKA

http://www.nebraskahistory.org

Nebraska State Historical Society

Figure 3.29

Nebraska State Historical Society

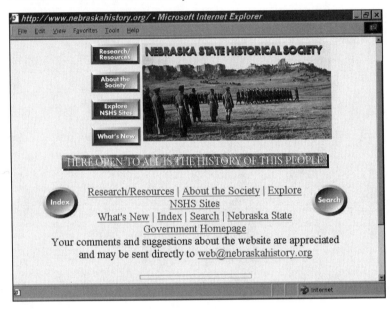

NEVADA

http://www.clan.lib.nv.us/docs/NSLA/nsla.htm

Nevada State Library and Archives

NEW HAMPSHIRE

http://www.state.nh.us/nhsl

New Hampshire State Library

NEW JERSEY

http://www.state.nj.us/state/darm/archives.html

New Jersey State Archives

NEW MEXICO

http://www.nmgs.org

New Mexico Genealogy Society

NEW YORK

http://www.sara.nysed.gov

New York State Archives and Records Administration

F i g u r e   3 . 3 0

New York State Archives and Records Administration

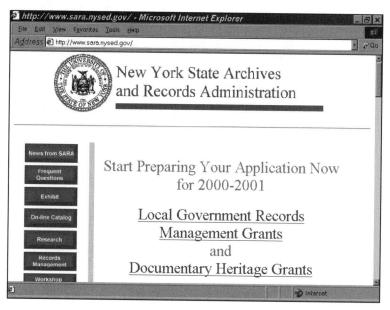

NORTH CAROLINA

http://statelibrary.dcr.state.nc.us/iss/gr/genealog.htm

State Library of North Carolina

NORTH DAKOTA

http://www.state.nd.us/hist/sal.htm

The North Dakota State Archives and Historical Resource Library

OHIO

http://www.ohiohistory.org

The Ohio Historical Society

Figure 3.31

Ohio Historical Society

OKLAHOMA

http://www.ok-history.mus.ok.us

Oklahoma Historical Society

OREGON

http://arcweb.sos.or.gov

Oregon State Archives

F i g u r e   3 . 3 2

Oregon State Archives

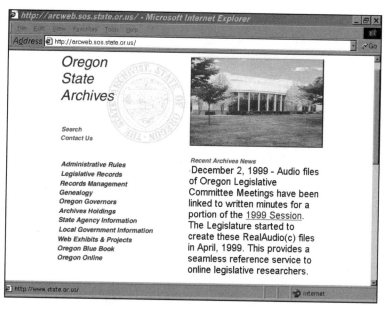

PENNSYLVANIA

http://www.state.pa.us/PA_Exec/Historical_Museum/DAM/genie1.htm

Pennsylvania State Archives

RHODE ISLAND

http://archives.state.ri.us

Rhode Island State Archives

SOUTH CAROLINA

http://www.state.sc.us/scdah/homepage.htm

The South Carolina Archives and History Center

SOUTH DAKOTA

http://www.state.sd.us/deca/cultural/archives.htm

South Dakota State Historical Society

F i g u r e   3 . 3 3

South Dakota State Archives

TENNESSEE

http://www.state.tn.us/sos/statelib/tslahome.htm
> *Tennessee State Library and Archives*

TEXAS

http://www.tsl.state.tx.us/lobby
> *Texas State Library and Archives Commission*

UTAH

http://www.archives.state.ut.us.
> *Utah State Archives*

F i g u r e   3 . 3 4

Utah Archives and Records Service

VERMONT

http://www.sec.state.vt.us/archives/archdex.htm
> *Vermont State Archives*

VIRGINIA

http://www.lva.lib.va.us
The Library of Virginia

Figure 3.35

The Library of Virginia

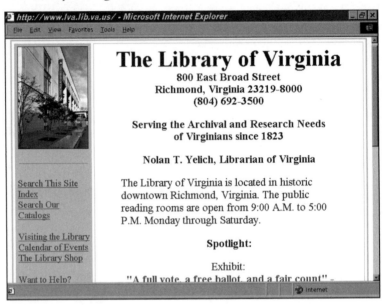

WASHINGTON

http://www.cwu.edu/~archives/genie.htm#BIRTHREC
Washington State Genealogy Society

WEST VIRGINIA

http://www.wvlc.wvnet.edu/history/wvsamenu.html
The West Virginia State Archives

WISCONSIN

http://www.wisc.edu/shs-archives/referenc.html
   The State Historical Society of Wisconsin, Archives Division

WYOMING

http://commerce.state.wy.us/cr/archives/county/county.htm
   Wyoming Archives, Records by County

F i g u r e 3 . 3 6

Wyoming Archives and Records by County

*"To know the road ahead,
ask those coming back."*

—Anonymous quote from the Internet

Federal Records

NATIONAL ARCHIVES AND RECORDS ADMINISTRATION (NARA)

http://www.nara.gov

Now that we've been to each state's archives, let's make a virtual visit to our national archives. Everyone has heard of the National Archives and Records Administration (NARA), but most people do not have a clear understanding of the agency's function. The NARA is an independent federal agency whose primary purpose is to manage and preserve our federal records, especially those that document the rights of American citizens. A few of the NARA's holdings include crucial historical documents like the Declaration of Independence, the Constitution of the United States, and the Bill of Rights.

The NARA is not like other genealogy-related Web sites. Currently, you will not find vast amounts of genealogy information there, but the government is committed to building a nationwide information network that will educate citizens about the NARA and its facilities, services, and holdings.

At the NARA's home page, click on Research Room, where you will find Quick Links to Genealogy & Family History. Since the NARA has very few actual records online, what you will find is how to locate information such as Immigration and

Naturalization Records, Federal Employee Records, and American Indian Records. The NARA is the official repository for military personnel who have been discharged from the U.S. Air Force, Army, Marine Corps, Navy, and Coast Guard. The site has instructions for ordering the paper records of military service and pension records held by the facility.

You can access the NARA records online through the NARA Archival Information Locator (NAIL). Read the information about searching the archives and see what you can find.

F i g u r e   3 . 3 7

The National Archives and Records Administration.

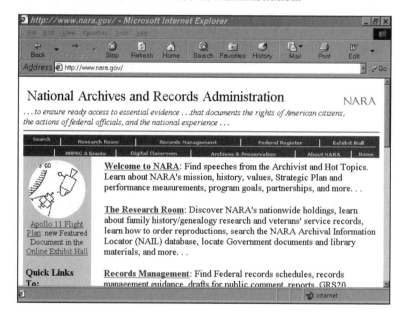

> *"The Heritage of the Past
> is in the Seed that brings forth
> the Harvest of the Future."*
>
> —carved in a stone flanking the
> National Archives building in Washington, D.C.

No traditional genealogy research would be complete without delving into census records, maps, and ships' lists. Where these kinds of searches are concerned, the Internet holds no bounds. Many rare documents are now being digitized and published on the Internet. The result is a wonderful opportunity for the average citizen to see things like handwritten census records and antique maps that would once have been reserved for those with physical access to museums and government holdings.

Traditional genealogy research might require the use of a magnifying glass to read the small text on paper documents. Small type and bad lighting will not affect your Internet searching ability. Now, with the help of your computer's Web browser, it is far easier to read records and find a single name out of thousands. Remember to use your Web browser's Find feature as you unearth the information in records like the ones listed here.

CENSUS RECORDS ONLINE

http://www.census-online.com

F i g u r e   3 . 3 8

Census Records Online.

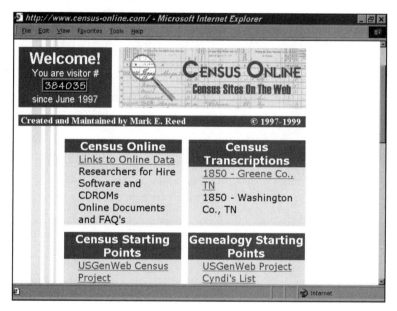

This Web site does not have all of the U.S. census records, nor, unfortunately, does any other single, online source. Don't try the U.S. Census Bureau's Web site, either. The federal government is not in the business of publishing census records for genealogy purposes. However, because Census Records Online is connected to U.S. GenWeb, we might eventually be able to see all census records on the Internet! Right now, Census Records Online is one of the biggest projects on the Internet. What you will find here is extremely useful, especially if you have ever tried to find census records through the genealogy section of your local library. It's a real treat to find the census record that you want online and be able to print it from your own computer. Most of the census schedules are housed at the county level. Many GenWeb volunteers have made diligent efforts to get the census schedules online. Currently, the only census records that are legally available to the public, which are online, are those dated 1920 and earlier.

Tip

Both Internet Explorer and Netscape Navigator have a Find function under the Edit button on the toolbar or within the browser. This little feature can save you hours of time and eyestrain, especially when you are researching census schedules, which are posted in very tiny type. If you have a census schedule on the screen, and you are looking for a particular surname, click on Find (or press Ctrl+F). Type in the surname and then click Find Next. If there are any matches on the page, the Find feature will locate and highlight them. Too bad looking at census schedules the old-fashioned way isn't this easy. *Any time* you come to a page with a tremendous amount of data and you need to find one word (like a surname), remember this feature. Practice using it and save your eyes!

F i g u r e   3 . 3 9

Using the "Find" feature of an Internet Web browser to search through online archives like census records.

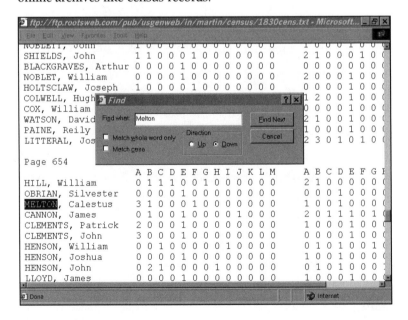

SOCIAL SECURITY DEATH INDEX

There are a few free Social Security Death Indexes on the Internet, but undoubtedly one of the best is offered through Ancestry. Go to the following Web site:

ANCESTRY'S SOCIAL SECURITY DEATH INDEX

http://www.ancestry.com/search/rectype/vital/ssdi/main.htm

F i g u r e   3 . 4 0

Ancestry's Social Security Death Index.

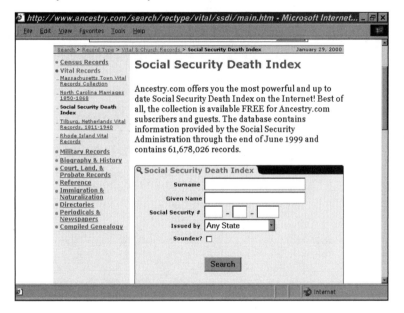

Type in the information you have about the person you are researching. The results give most researchers new information to go on.

The results from a search will produce Name, Birth Date, Death Date, Last Known Residence, Last Benefit Location, and Social Security Number. If you want a hard copy of your findings, there is an option you can select that will allow you to print a preformatted letter from your computer. The letter will contain your request for the information you need and the address to which you will mail the letter—all you have to do is add your postal address, phone number, and signature. You should also date the letter and make a copy for your records. Getting this information has never been easier!

"Theory of relativity: if you go back far enough, we're all related."

—Anonymous quote from the Internet

Maps

COLOR LANDFORM ATLAS
OF THE UNITED STATES

http://fermi.jhuapl.edu/states/states.html

For each state in the country, there is a wonderfully detailed 1895 map showing county borders, railroads, towns, and bodies of water. These maps were scanned from an actual 1895 atlas, and the images are large and legible. Maps are important genealogy tools because they help us determine the origins of our ancestors. County boundaries change while a country is still forming, and inaccurate information can lead us to search in the wrong county or township and waste valuable time. Each time you access one of these maps, it will take a minute or two for even the fastest computer to pull the Web page up, but it will be well worth the wait. Maps can give genealogists valuable information such as county boundaries. Knowing which county a family resided in, especially during the years when boundaries changed frequently, could help the genealogist locate vital records. Maps can also show possible family migration patterns, taking into account where the family lived and the growth of that area over a period of time.

DIGITAL IMAGING INITIATIVE/UNIVERSITY OF ILLINOIS AT URBANA-CHAMPAIGN

http://images.grainger.uiuc.edu

When you reach the home page of the Digital Imaging Initiative, click on Images. This will take you to a page of links to eighty-four maps that show North America and the Northwest Territory from 1650 to 1994. All of the maps are from the Map and Geography Library and the Rare Book and Special Collections Library at the University of Illinois at Urbana-Champaign.

THE PERRY-CASTAÑEDA LIBRARY MAP COLLECTION

http://www.lib.utexas.edu/Libs/PCL/Map_collection/histus.html

The Perry-Castañeda Library Map Collection through the University of Texas at Austin has probably the most complete collection of historical maps on the Internet. This Web site offers more than 700 maps, including historical city maps and maps showing Early Indian Tribes, Exploration and Settlement, Territorial Growth, National Historic Parks, Battlefields and Memorials. The collection has a link to other map Web sites, should you not find what you're looking for here.

JOHN ROBERTSON'S MAP COLLECTION

http://www.shelby.net/shelby/jr/

This Web site contains a collection of 1895 county maps, courtesy of Pam Rietsch. Most of the maps on this Web site have direct links to U.S. GenWeb. Even though it's smaller than the other map sites listed here, don't miss out on a good thing.

F i g u r e   3 . 4 1

An 1847 Illinois county boundary map linked to John Robertson's Map Collection.

Military Resources

Although there is no all-encompassing Web site for military records, the following list contains some very good ones. They might guide you to specific family information or even provide addresses and phone numbers of agencies that can help you find a record of military service. Visit these sites often, because these Web sites are updated frequently with new members and information.

LINEAGES MILITARY RESEARCH ROOM

http://www.lineages.com/military

The Military Research Room at Lineages is a very user-friendly Web site, so it is a good place to begin military research. Lineages (**http://www.lineages.com**) does not have as many actual records as some of the bigger sites, like Ancestry and Family Tree Maker, but it does have some wonderful links to online military information.

AMERICAN CIVIL WAR DATABASE

http://www.civilwardata.com

F i g u r e   3 . 4 2

The American Civil War Database.

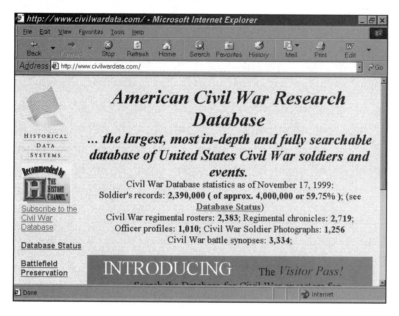

This service charges a small fee, but the database contains records for almost two and a half million soldiers. You can conduct a brief free search, to see if your ancestor is listed within the database, by following these instructions:

1. On the left-hand side of the home page, click on Subscribe to the Civil War Database. You will not be subscribing to the American Civil War Database; you'll just get to the next step.

2. When you get to the next page, click on American Civil War Database Demonstration at the bottom of the left-hand column of the page.

3. This will take you to the Demo page. Near the bottom, amid other text, you will see highlighted Personnel and Officer directories. By clicking on either one, you can look for an ancestor.

Since you are not subscribing to the database, but using this system to see whether a particular person has been entered in it, you can see results that include First, Middle and Last name, Residence, State, Occupation, Enlisted Rank, Enlisted Age, and Enlisted Date. Later, if you do decide to subscribe to the American Civil War Database, you will be able to retrieve other information, like Regiments, Companies, Rank, Promotions, and Transfers. Occasionally, search results may also yield POW information, statistics on wounded personnel, and how and where a given soldier exited the military—Discharge, Desertion, Muster Out, Death (including the cause of death, if available). Some records might even include Birthplace, Occupation, and Physical Description.

Although you will have to pay the fee to reap the full benefits of this database, depending on what information you are seeking, the price is reasonable.

KOREAN CONFLICT CASUALTY SITE

http://www.nara.gov/nara/electronic/kcasal.html

This site records only casualties of the Korean Conflict. It is a branch of the U.S. National Archives and has a searchable database. Casualties can be found by last name or home of the person you are searching for.

POW/MIA HOME PAGE

http://lcweb2.loc.gov/pow/powhome.html

The POW/MIA home page is another government Web site. It, too, has a searchable database and offers the user an opportunity to obtain free microfilm records.

THE AMERICAN WAR LIBRARY

http://members.aol.com/veterans

Figure 3.43

The American War Library.

This is the Cyndi's List of military Web sites, except that it is not the easiest site to navigate. There is a searchable index, but the veteran you are looking for has to be registered (if still living). You will be able to access information about deceased veterans, because the site lists thousands of government records like Missing-In-Action and P.O.W. files. There are other records, such as written documentation from war correspondents. In order to use all areas of the site, you will need to download free software from the site and install it on your computer. This will enable you to do a complete search of the database. At the bottom of the page, however, you will find other veterans' and military Web sites. Clicking on one of these sites will give you hundreds of places to search.

THE WALL ON THE WEB

http://grunt.space.swri.edu/thewall/thewallm.html

Figure 3.44
The Wall on the Web Home Page.

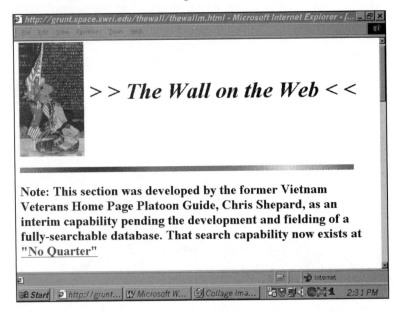

This is the Vietnam Memorial on the Web. The Web site has a searchable database that returns an abundance of information on the personal and military records of individual soldiers. More detailed information about Vietnam War casualties can be found at Lineages Military Research Room, mentioned earlier in this section.

A BARREL OF GENEALOGY LINKS

http://cpcug.org/user/jlacombe/mark.html

This Web site is owned and maintained by John Lacombe. There are hundreds of links from this page; however, the most useful resource is the listing of more than one hundred Civil War links near the bottom of his home page. Whether you're doing genealogy research or just a history buff, these links will keep you busy for hours.

Tip

If you buy an inexpensive dot matrix printer, it will pay for itself quickly. When you really begin to delve deeply into genealogy on the Internet, you are sure to do a massive amount of printing. You might tell yourself, at first, that you will be selective about what you print, but in the end you will print just about everything. It's much cheaper to print on a dot matrix than an inkjet, whose cartridges are expensive. I learned this the hard way after printing out a couple hundred pages of my family history information. I soon hooked up my old dot matrix and bought an A/B switch so I could use either printer. I still use the inkjet when I want good quality, but I kick on the dot matrix if I'm going to print up twenty or thirty pages of family history data.

What happens when you can't find what you are looking for on the Internet? Well, you can always write away for the records you need. Before the Internet, you could spend a phenomenal amount of time and money just calling directory assistance for long-distance phone numbers. Now, with the click of a mouse, you can retrieve not only phone numbers, but postal addresses, e-mail addresses, and fax numbers for courthouses and health care offices across the country.

Listed here are a few sources you can write to, if need be, for vital record information. Even though they have similar and sometimes overlapping information, I mention them individually because each one has its own unique features.

Vital Records

VITAL RECORDS

http://vitalrec.com/index.html

> This Web site lists offices and agencies you can write to for vital information (births, deaths, marriages, and divorces) at the state, territory, and county level in the United States. The site also notes any fees charged by the government agencies or record offices. Most fees are nominal.

VITALCHEK NETWORK

http://www.vitalchek.com

F i g u r e   3 . 4 5

Vitalchek.

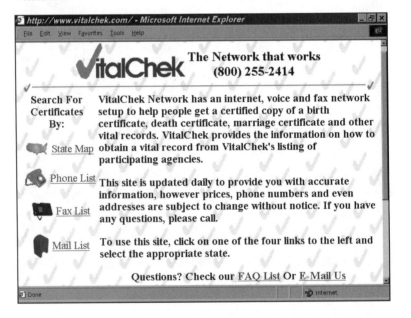

VitalChek Network lets users obtain certified copies of birth certificates, death certificates, marriage certificates, and other vital records by means of voice mail and fax. This service costs more than going through courthouses and health departments, because you are paying for the convenience of ordering by phone or fax. If your time is scarce, though, this service might help you make the best use of it.

NATIONAL CENTER FOR HEALTH STATISTICS

http://209.67.208.64/vital_records_services.html

F i g u r e   3 . 4 6

The National Center for Health Statistics (NCHS) is the Government's principal vital and health statistics agency. The NCHS provides links to each state's vital records office.

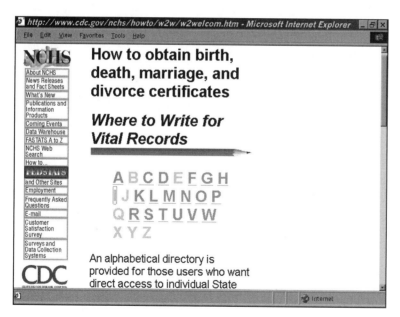

From this U.S. State Department Web site, you can request official birth, death, and marriage certificates and also military personnel records. Printable order forms make requesting these records a breeze.

When writing to any of the agencies listed here, it is extremely helpful to follow some basic criteria.

◆ When no order form is available, type your request, if possible. Keep it simple and precise.

◆ If you must write your request by hand, *print it*, to avoid any misinterpretations of names or other data.

◆ Make each request an individual order (one per envelope) to avoid any confusion with family surnames, and be sure to include all the information that agency personnel will need to search the appropriate record. List complete names, nicknames, alternate spellings, and relevant dates, if known.

◆ Always remember to send the exact payment that is required, and be aware that some places will accept only money orders. Always include a self-addressed stamped envelope (SASE).

More specifically, requests for birth certificate should include:

◆ First, middle, and last name of person

◆ Date of birth (month, day, year)

◆ Birthplace

◆ Mother's maiden name

◆ Father's name

◆ A note saying that this is for genealogy research

◆ Your name, address, driver's license number, and state in which your license was issued. (Yes, you may be asked for your driver's license number!) If you include your phone number, it might expedite matters should a question arise.

◆ Your signature, which is usually needed for any transaction involving official records.

Requests for death certificates should include:

◆ First, middle, and last name of deceased

◆ Date of birth (month, day, year)

◆ Date of death (month, day, year)

◆ Place of death (city and state)

◆ A note saying that this is for genealogy research

◆ Your name, address, driver's license number, state in which your license was issued, and, if you like, your phone number

◆ Your signature

Requests for marriage certificates should include:

- ◆ First, middle, and last name of husband
- ◆ First, middle, and last (maiden) name of wife
- ◆ Date of marriage
- ◆ Place of marriage (city and state)
- ◆ A note saying that this is for genealogy research
- ◆ Your name, address, phone number (optional), driver's license number and state
- ◆ Your signature

If you do not have all these details when you order a record, don't be alarmed. The main idea is to give the records clerk or researcher as much information as you have. Always remember to date your request and keep a copy or record of it. You might use a correspondence log, which is simply a record of the letters you send, to which agencies, when, and for what information.

> *"Genealogy; where you confuse the dead and irritate the living."*
>
> —Anonymous quote from the Internet

Libraries

The library Web sites listed here will guide you to an abundance of information, from family histories and biographies to census records and military history. Some libraries will look things up for you for free. If you are fortunate enough to find one, you could send them a small donation. The majority of the libraries do charge for lookups, but the fees are usually small. A few repositories do not do lookups at all; but if you go to their Web sites and look through their holdings, you will see whether they have the reference materials you need.

FAMILY HISTORY CENTERS

http://www.genhomepage.com/FHC/fhc.html

This site will give you the address of the Family History Center (FHC) nearest you. As you know from our earlier discussion, the Church of Jesus Christ of Latter-day Saints (the Mormon Church) of Salt Lake City, Utah, owns one of the most extensive genealogical databases worldwide. Many of the resources in this database are shared with Family History Centers. Some FHCs have their own Web sites, which you can access by clicking on their link. Listed along with the FHC addresses are their phone numbers and hours.

GENEALOGY LIBRARIES IN THE UNITED STATES

http://www.greenheart.com/rdietz/gen_libs.htm

F i g u r e 3 . 4 7

Find a genealogy library near you with this directory of libraries with genealogical collections in the U.S..

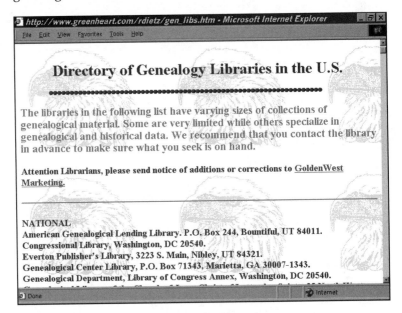

This is a link from a larger Web site, Golden West Marketing, at **http://www.greenheart.com/rdietz/index.html**. This smaller site lists hundreds of addresses for genealogy libraries across the country, categorized by state. Hyperlinks will take you directly to the libraries that have home pages.

Tip

Look for your family tree on CD-ROM at your nearest genealogy library. As more and more libraries offer the free use of computers with access to the Internet, more are also acquiring family tree indexes on CD-ROM. Companies like Family Tree Maker have created these CD-ROMs, which contain family trees that have been compiled from government records and individuals. Because genealogy CD-ROMs can cost $30 to $50 each, finding them at the library can save you a bundle. You might consider making a small donation to any library that supplies them, as a gesture of gratitude.

THE LIBRARY OF CONGRESS STATE LIBRARIES

http://lcweb.loc.gov/global/library/statelib.html

Figure 3.48

The Library of Congress State Libraries

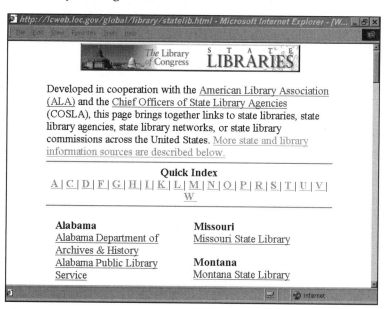

This site contains a complete state-by-state listing of links to state libraries online. State libraries are a wonderful source of biographies and regional history.

DIRECTORY OF U.S. PUBLIC LIBRARIES WITH WEB SITES

http://www.capecod.net/epl/public_libraries.html

This Web site offers links to U.S. public libraries that have Web sites. As of this writing, the site lists more than 700 libraries. These are not genealogy libraries, but some of them do have genealogy-related materials. Read the short description with each Web site; it should describe the library holdings. If you are still in doubt, go to the library's home page, look for its e-mail address, and pose your question to the head librarian.

Books

Save yourself hours of investigating family records by looking for research that has already been done. Someone you might never have heard of could already have compiled many generations of your family tree—but where do you look? Check out genealogy libraries, ask your relatives, and search the Internet. There are many publishers who specialize in collecting and publishing family histories. I don't have room to list more than a few, but their Web sites contain large holdings of family history books and region-specific history books you can purchase.

These book companies are in the business of collecting family history books for reprint purposes. If you are fortunate to find a book containing some of your family history, the company will make a copy of the book for you. Prices are usually based on the number of pages (price per page), the quality of paper, and whether you want the copy to be bound as a paperback or hardback book. Copyright laws are adhered to because these companies either purchase the rights to the books or the books are in the public domain.

If you cannot find the book you are looking for on the Web sites below, try e-mailing the sites with a specific book request. These vendors are constantly adding new books to their lists, and they might have more on hand than the ones posted on their site.

YE OLDE GENEALOGIE SHOPPE©

http://www.yogs.com

Ye Olde Genealogie Shoppe© has been around as a mail-order service for genealogy research supplies since 1974. In the past few years, this business has been growing on the Web, selling its genealogy books, forms, charts, maps, CD-ROMs, and seminars. The states for which it has the most reference materials are Indiana, Illinois, Kentucky, Maryland, Ohio, North Carolina, Pennsylvania, and Tennessee. Ye Olde Genealogie Shoppe© also sells books and publications relating to New England genealogy, military, maps, and much more. This is a great place for the beginner to pick up kits. Be sure to check out the bargain section.

HIGGINSON BOOK COMPANY

http://www.higginsonbooks.com

Higginson Book Company is my favorite genealogy publisher on the Internet. It offers more than 10,000 titles and a search engine that lets you look for specific books. Each book is listed with a brief description and is categorized for easier searching. Higginson's list includes not only family history books, but also local and county histories, books on the military, foreign countries, emigrants, heraldry, and marriages, and general reference books and research aids.

Even if you are lucky enough to find a book that traces your family history, your search has not ended. How long ago was the book compiled? Has anyone updated it? How many new family members have been born, or branches added? Genealogy is more than just making a record of the past; it is also *keeping* a record of the present for future generations.

The Melting Pot

In the United States, we share a very diverse heritage. The phrase "melting pot" has been coined to represent the uniqueness of our country. Nowhere in the world will one find so many languages, religions, and cultures represented under one flag.

Before Lincoln's presidency, immigrants migrated to the U.S. from Germany, Ireland, Great Britain, Sweden, Norway, and the Netherlands. Later, Irish immigrants, escaping the potato famine in Ireland, would seek refuge on American shores. The discovery of gold in the 1840s brought new Chinese and Latin American immigrants to this country.

Through the 1800s and 1900s, immigrants continued to arrive in the United States from Scandinavia, Japan, Canada, and many other countries. Most of these immigrant ancestors can be found on the ship lists in this section. Another good place to locate these ancestors is the U.S. GenWeb site located in Step 3 of this book. This section also addresses the challenging genealogical searches that Native Americans and African-Americans must undertake to find their roots. The Web sites listed here are among the best starting points.

Emigration/Immigration Records and Ship Lists

ELLIS ISLAND

http://www.ellisisland.org

Currently, you will not find on the Internet any comprehensive files concerning the immigrants who came through Ellis Island upon entering this country. You will find information on a new American Family Immigration History Center being constructed within the Ellis Island Immigration Museum. This project will eventually digitize and enter into a computer database the records of more than 17 million people who immigrated through the port of New York from 1892 to 1924. There are also plans for making the Immigration Arrival Records available via the Internet in the future. For more information on this project, visit the Web site.

Figure 3.49

The Ellis Island Immigration Museum Web site.

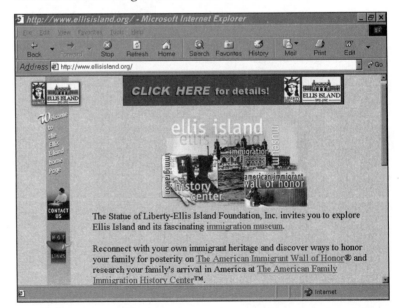

THE OLIVE TREE GENEALOGY

http://www.rootsweb.com/~ote

searchable database

This is an amazing place! It was one of the first Web sites that truly surprised me in my genealogy research. The Olive Tree Genealogy contains categorized lists of ships, and the site has a new search engine as well. Most of the lists are reproduced just as they were recorded. They contain dates and ports of departure, dates and ports of arrival, and the date that the ship first sailed. Passenger lists record the names and ages of passengers—all men, women, and children on the ship during each voyage. Some lists also record deaths that took place at sea. Here you will find passenger lists from ships sailing to the New World, beginning with the Santa Maria in 1492 and ending with the Brig Fortunato, an Italian immigrant ship that sailed in 1949.

A MAYFLOWER AND NEW ENGLAND STUDY

http://www.mayflowerfamilies.com

This is definitely a two-for-one Web site, rich with far more information than the data gathered about the Mayflower and its passengers. If you have an interest in early Colonial life, take a virtual tour of this comprehensive library of early American life.

THE MAYFLOWER DATABASE
http://users.voidnet.com/lssteadman/

If you have wondered whether any of your ancestors came over on the Mayflower, The Mayflower Database is a marvelous tool for finding out. Because the database is so large, it will take a minute or two (or three) to load, even on the fastest computer! Be patient, because it is definitely worth the wait. The Web site's search engine lets you search by full name, surname, or Soundex. Once you find the person you are looking for, you can view family group sheets, ancestor charts, or descendent charts for that person.

Native American Research

Numerous Web sites publish Native American family histories. Still, these lineages are probably the most difficult to trace on the Internet as well as through other avenues. As with all genealogy research, start with what you know. I recommend searching within broad-based genealogy databases like U.S. GenWeb before conducting a more specific search. First, search the Internet by geographic area, then search for the name of a family related to yours by marriage, and then search for the names of specific individuals. GenForum, which is discussed in the next chapter, has some very good bulletin boards for meeting other researchers and exchanging information. Other Web sites listed here will provide you primarily with contact names and with many people who can help you in your search.

GENFORUM/SPECIFIC TOPICS/ AMERICAN INDIAN

http://www.genforum.genealogy.com/ai

> You will use this forum just as you would use any of the others at GenForum. For information on GenForum, see Section One of the next chapter, Genealogy Bulletin Boards and Posting.

PAST TRACKER

http://www.harborside.com/home/r/rice/index.html

> This service specializes in searching for Native American records, for which it charges a small fee.

HOMETOWN AOL

http://hometown.aol.com/bbbenge/front.html

F i g u r e   3 . 5 0

AOL Hometown Native American genealogy.

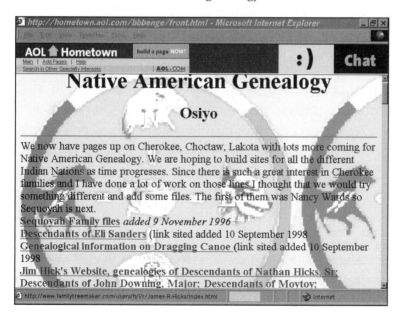

This Web site is one of the best all-around resources for Native American genealogy. It provides links to many Web sites, most of them the home pages of AOL users. You do not need to be a member of AOL to access these pages, which sometimes have as much useful information as Web sites operated by organizations and government offices. When individuals maintain Web sites, they usually volunteer their valuable time, pouring heart and soul into it. More often than not, they are experts in their specific field of study. In the case of Native American genealogy, volunteer researchers have posted a tremendous amount of information for public use and exchange.

African-American Research

African-American genealogy research is becoming easier with a surge of new sites dedicated to this purpose. New information is being processed and posted to the Internet daily. Fortunately, more people have seen a demand for this information and are willing to spend the time and effort to publish it on the Internet.

If your genealogy research so far has brought you only births, deaths, marriages, and church records, you can now go deeper. For example, at the sites mentioned below, you will find records from slave ships, Black newspapers, and runaway slave ads. In addition, the U.S. census records show free Blacks in records from as early as 1790. The Census Bureau has records of former slaves from 1870. Most slave owners kept very good records, such as plantation records, insurance records, sharecropping records, breeding records, and freedom (or manumission) papers. Many such records can be found on the Internet at some of the sites listed here, as well as at broader Web sites like U.S. GenWeb and RootsWeb.

CHRISTINE'S GENEALOGY WEB SITE

http://www.ccharity.com

Figure 3.51

Christine's Genealogy Web site.

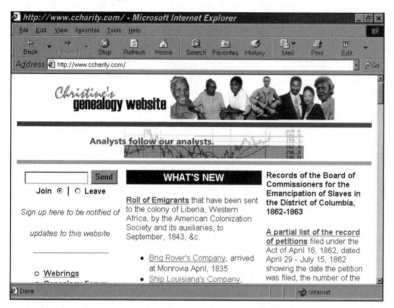

This Web site, created by Christine Charity, is loaded with "bells and whistles"—message boards, home pages, census research, fugitive slave cases, cemeteries, wills, obituaries, archives, and too much more to mention here. The *best* feature of this Web site is the search engine midway down the home page. It will search all of the records contained in or linked to this site. I typed in a common surname, Smith, and got ninety-five results, ranging from actual family trees to Smiths listed in census schedules and emigration records. Your search for anything related to African-American genealogy should begin here!

THE FREEDMEN'S BUREAU ONLINE

http://www.freedmensbureau.com

Here's another Web site maintained by Christine Charity. It contains a fantastic collection of records pertaining to marriages, indenture bonds, orphan lists, and diaries. The Freedmen's Bureau Online is a compilation of records from the National Archives. Links to records are sorted by state. This is another great place for researching African-American roots.

LEST WE FORGET

http://www.coax.net/people/LWF/default.htm

Bennie J. McRae, Jr., the researcher and site manager for Lest We Forget, accepts submissions from volunteer researchers and publishes the findings. The primary focus of this Web site is African-American genealogy, and the majority of the site is a series of links directing you to online sources.

AFRIGENEAS

http://www.afrigeneas.com

Figure 3.52

AfriGeneas Home Page.

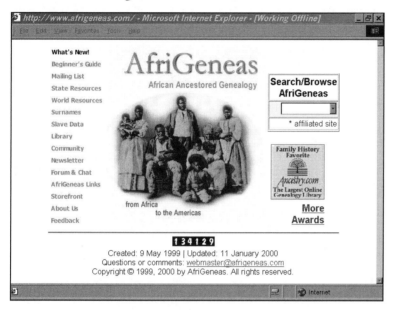

AfriGeneas has the oldest African-American Genealogy Mailing List on the Internet. One of the site's best features is the Mailing List Archives, a record that categorizes all of the information in the mailing list by the month and year. A search engine makes it a breeze to look through the archives for surnames. With similarities to the U.S. GenWeb Project, AfriGeneas has begun setting up state Web sites exclusively for African-American family history research. As of this writing, only Alabama and

South Carolina have records online and twenty-six other states have Web sites under construction; however, given the success of U.S. GenWeb, I feel that this site will also be a major contributor to the online genealogy community. In an area of the Web site titled New and Ongoing Projects, volunteers work on endeavors like African-American Cemeteries Online and Slave Ship Manifests Database. The volunteers have eight other major projects underway and eleven proposed projects.

SECTION FOUR:

Adoption Records

The Internet is flooded with adoption resources, or registries, which connect adopted people with their birth families and vice-versa. If you already have information about earlier generations of your birth family, you can best follow its trail through Web sites like RootsWeb (mentioned earlier in this Step), which can put you in touch with others who have researched your family tree. The Web sites listed below focus only on birth parents and adopted children. All are adoption registries and when you register with one of them, you are saying that you are willing to be contacted by a child you gave up or by the birth parent who placed you for adoption. Some of the registries have searchable databases organized by location and date of birth.

Here are some excellent places to begin your adoption research:

ADOPTION.COM

http://www.adoption.com

Figure 3.53

Adoption.com.

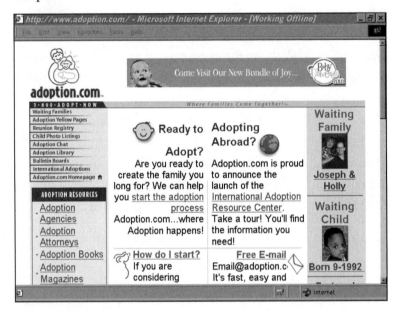

Adoption.com not only contains an adoption registry, but it is a virtual library of resources for anyone searching for their biological roots or branches. The site has links connecting to adoption agencies, attorneys, books, and information on international adoption.

REUNION REGISTRY

http://www.reunionregistry.com

Reunion Registry is the largest free mutual consent reunion registry on the Internet. Anyone can search for adoptees, biological parents, old friends, lost loves, missing relatives, military buddies, classmates, teachers, or almost anyone. Adoptees and birth parents who wish to search this site should complete the registration online. Then they can proceed to the adoption section of the registry and check for a potential match. Be aware that adoptees are listed by their date of birth, city, and state of birth; birth family members are listed by the date, city, and state of birth of the adoptee they are seeking.

Figure 3.54

The Reunion Registry Web site.

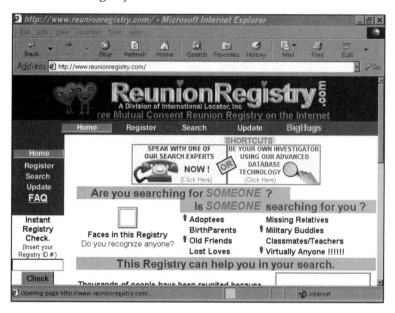

BIRTH QUEST

http://www.birthquest.org

Birth Quest is another very good adoption registry. The site has its own search engine and will search through a wide range of criteria, including birth dates, birth mother's name, hospital of birth, and adoptee's city of birth. As of this writing, there are more than 22,000 registrations on file with Birth Quest.

Odds & Ends of Genealogy Web Sites (Mostly Odds!)

The reason I say "mostly odds"—well, just take a look at the names of the Web sites listed here and you'll soon get the picture. Don't dismiss these Web sites as fluff, however. A few are very useful, and some are among my favorite places to visit on the Internet. Even though genealogy is a serious hobby, Web sites like the ones listed here make room for our sense of humor. Sit back and delight in the variety of information on the Web.

CEMETERY JUNCTION

http://www.daddezio.com/cemetery

This Web site is a wonderful resource if you are trying to locate a cemetery anywhere in this country. As of this writing, more than 13,000 cemeteries are listed—not all of them, but the managers of this site are making a valiant effort in that direction. The Web site's search engine allows the user to look for a cemetery by name or state. The site is now attempting to add cemeteries from other countries to their ever-growing list.

FIND A GRAVE

http://www.findagrave.com

Figure 3.55
Find A Grave.

This site is one of several links from Cemetery Junction. It's listed separately here, because it deserves a category all by itself. A man named Jim Tipton created and maintains this site. On the home page, Jim says, "I collect dirt from the graves of noteworthy people.... This is a source for where such people are buried." You can search for gravesites by the name, location or claim to fame of the person buried there. I found my own distant cousin, General John Pershing, at this site. If there's anyone famous or notorious in your family, chances are, you'll dig them up here.

> *"Genealogy is not fatal,*
> *but it is a grave disease."*
>
> —Anonymous quote from the Internet

INTERNATIONAL BLACK SHEEP
SOCIETY OF GENEALOGISTS

http://homepages.rootsweb.com/~blksheep

Figure 3.56

The Black Sheep Society Web site.

When you enter this Web site, turn up the volume on your computer's speakers—you don't want to miss the sheep! Jeff Scism is the Flock Master of the site, and he will publish the "black sheep" history of anyone who wants to become a member. As with any organization, you must meet the qualifications for membership.

For membership in the IBSS, you must have an ancestor who qualifies as a "dastardly, infamous individual of public knowledge and ill-repute in their family...within one degree of consanguinity of their direct lines. This individual must have been pilloried in disgrace for acts of a significantly anti-social nature."

There's usually one bad apple on every family tree, so check out this Web site. The International Black Sheep Society also has a high-volume mailing list for a wide variety of genealogy-related topics. You can also find genealogy tips and Black Sheep histories in the site's chat area. Finding both your inlaws and outlaws on the Internet can be fun.

U.S. SURNAME DISTRIBUTION MAP

http://www.primenet.com/~hamrick/names

Figure 3.57

A U.S. Surname Distribution Map displaying the frequency of the surname "Melton" according to 1880 census records.

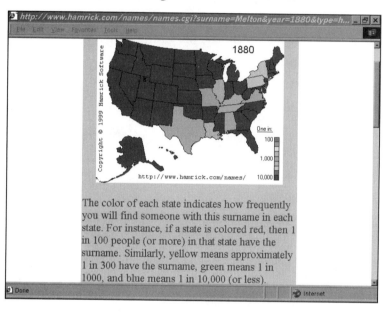

This is a wonderful tool for any genealogist. When you type a surname into this computer program, a U. S. map will come up that displays a color-coded graph showing the geographic distribution of people with that surname. The information used at this site was gathered from U.S. census schedules from 1850, 1880, and 1920. Information in phone books from 1990 was also used. The Census details comprised a sampling of one in one hundred names, so the 1990 statistics are most accurate. I typed in my maiden name, Melton, for the census of 1850.

The map showed that the highest concentrations of Meltons were in Alabama, Missouri, and Indiana. By the census of 1880, however, the majority of Meltons lived in Texas, Louisiana, Missouri, and Virginia. This database does not contain every name in a given census schedule, but it does index more than 50,000 of the most common names in the country. This map is great if you are trying to pinpoint when and where a family entered the country and possibly to trace the migration pattern of people with that family name.

PRESIDENTIAL GENEALOGIES ON THE WEB

http://homepages.rootsweb.com/~godwin/reference/prez.html

Figure 3.58

Presidential Genealogies on the web.

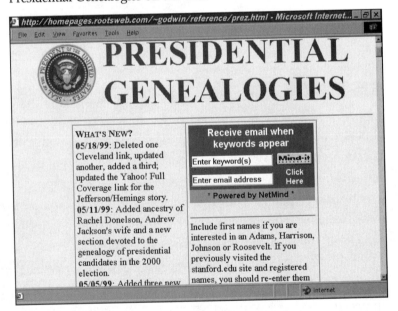

Here's your chance for a claim to fame. You can find U. S. Presidential family histories from Washington to Clinton, including the families of the First Ladies. RootsWeb sponsors this site, which is maintained by Jennifer Gordon. This site is full of links to other Presidential databases, history pages, and biographical information. Books and CDs containing Presidential family histories are available for purchase at this Web site.

> *"The fastest way to trace your family tree is to run for public office."*
>
> —Anonymous quote from the Internet

OLD BUNCOMBE COUNTY GENEALOGY SOCIETY, INC., OF NORTH CAROLINA
http://main.nc.us/OBCGS/research.htm

This definitely qualifies for the "odds" category. The Old Buncombe County Genealogy Society has a Web page like many others, with plenty of genealogy data at the state and local levels; but what makes it so interesting is its wealth of *unusual* information.

Here are just a few examples: Ahnentafel (the German numbering system for an ancestral table), Kinship, Gravestone Symbols, Old Time Measurements, Calendars (Julian, Gregorian, Old Style, New Style, Revolutionary), and Genealogy Abbreviations (and their meanings). Don't neglect to explore this incredibly helpful Web site. The reference information is priceless to any researcher.

GENEALOGICAL WEB SITES WATCHDOG

http://www.ancestordetective.com/watchdog.htm

F i g u r e   3 . 5 9

Genealogical Web Site Watchdog.

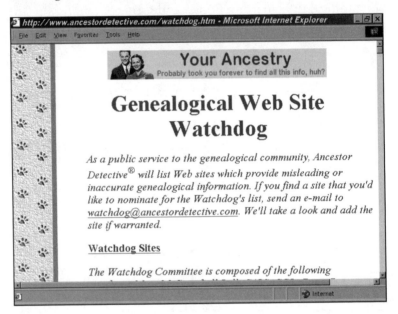

This is a Web page from Ancestor Detective. The site investigates and publishes Web sites that have inaccurate or misleading genealogy information. The Watchdog committee is composed of six members, all from the Association of Professional Genealogists. They provide this Web site as a public service to the genealogy community.

Are you ready to go even deeper? Move to Step 4.

Step 4

Connecting Online

Lots of other genealogy researchers just like you are out there in cyberspace, eager to share information with you and to help you have better success. Here is where to find them.

SECTION ONE:
Genealogy Forums

Picture a bulletin board at the local grocery store. Now, instead of the usual mish-mash of items for sale, services offered, help-wanted ads, event announcements, and lost-and-found notices, picture an entire wall of neatly organized genealogy information. Now, picture several such "walls" online.

With millions of Web sites in cyberspace, it would be nearly impossible to have a central bulletin board. Yet the Internet is full of bulletin boards for almost every topic imaginable. These are also referred to as forums, message boards, or query boards. The genealogy community has made wonderful use of the Internet to connect researchers with common information. This would be impossible without the thousands of genealogy forums—especially since many of them index and archive their information, and some have built-in search engines as well.

To find out what a genealogy bulletin board looks like and how to use it, let's visit one called GenForum. This is not only my favorite genealogy forum, it is probably the most organized of the hundreds, perhaps thousands, on the Internet. It is certainly one of the largest, as you will soon discover. If you want to find other genealogy bulletin boards, after you have visited GenForum, go to the genealogy section of your favorite Web directory (such as Yahoo! or AltaVista). For a more comprehensive discussion of Web directories, see Step 2, Section Two.

Now let's go to:

GENFORUM

http://genforum.genealogy.com

F i g u r e   4 . 1

The GenForum Web site.

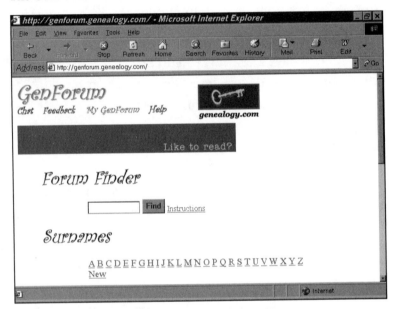

When you get to GenForum, you will not see a registration or sign-up area, because this wonderful resource is free to everyone. It is also very user-friendly. At the top of the page you will see Chat, Feedback, My Genforum, and Help. Below that there is usually an advertisement. You will also notice that GenForum is sponsored by Genealogy.com, another great genealogy Web directory. Directly below the advertisement, you will see Forum Finder and its search box.

There are two ways to access the surname you are researching. You can type a surname in the Forum Finder search box, and GenForum will take you directly to the bulletin boards. Or you can go to the alphabetized Surname index and search the list of names. The Surname index is a great way to find a specific bulletin board if you're not sure of a surname's spelling or if you are researching an unusual surname. Looking for the Soundex equivalent of that name might give you a lead.

What happens if you do not find a forum for your surname? Suppose you have typed it into the Forum Finder, and the response says:

> No matches were found for (name).

> If you would like to see the surname you searched for included in our Web site, please complete our New Forum Application.

Just click on "New Forum Application" and fill it out. Within a few weeks to a month, a new forum will be started for the surname you specified. You will receive an e-mail message giving you the forum's Web address (URL). Then you can go there and start posting. Before you post *anything*, though, be sure to read the rest of this section, because it offers step-by-step instructions on how and what to post to get the most responses.

Figure 4.2

The GenForum New Forum Application screen.

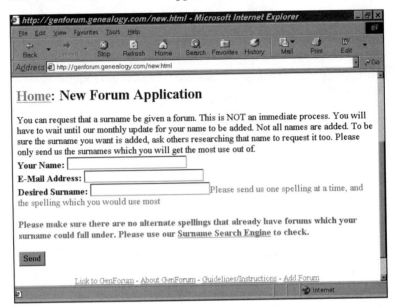

To see what a forum looks like, go ahead and look up a family surname that you are researching. Or if you prefer to follow along with me, here's an example: When I type the surname Tomey in the Forum Finder, the Tomey Family Genealogy Forum comes up. When you do this with a name you are researching, and you scroll down the page, your forum will look something like this:

Figure 4.3

The Tomey Family Genealogy Forum.

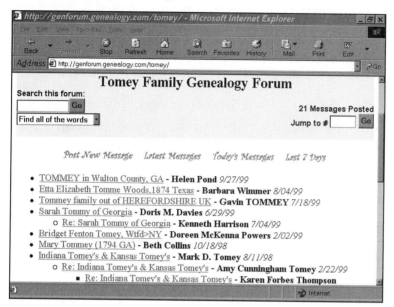

Here is how to read postings like the one above and use them effectively. Home and Surnames will take you to the GenForum home page or back to the Surname index at any time. Beneath the name of any specific forum is a notice that says "includes all obvious variations." If my surname were Tommy rather than Tomey, I could still post to this forum, although it would be better to find a Tommy forum. Many families changed the spelling of their names after arriving in the United States. Keep in mind that some of your ancestors might be found in other forums.

In Figure 4.3, notice the posting, Indiana Tomey's & Kansas Tomey's. This posting was made by Mark D. Tomey on 8/11/98, and you can see the entire post by clicking on this link. Responses to postings look like the line beneath his posting. Each response is indented. Sometimes you will see a response to a response, and this example also shows you what this looks like.

Follow the two steps below to post on GenForum—or any other genealogy bulletin board. Your odds of making contact with other researchers will increase greatly if you use this method.

At GenForum's home page, go to the forum for the name you are researching. To post a message, click on Post Message beneath the Family Genealogy Forum, or scroll all the way to the bottom of the page and click on the bar for posting a new message. This will take you to the posting page, where you will be asked for your name, e-mail address, and subject. You will learn how to set up your own e-mail accounts later in this chapter, but for now, let's get started on posting by following these steps:

1. **Subject line**. This should include the name of the person or family you are researching. If you are looking for an individual, include first, middle, and last names and any aliases he or she might have used. Also include the city and state and any dates that pertain to what you are searching for.

   The more information you post in the Subject line, the better chance you have of connecting to researchers. Use abbreviations to squeeze in the greatest amount of information.

Here is an example of what the subject line of a posting will look like:

George Washington Melton d:1903 KY > IN wife / V. Pershing

If you want to show that the person moved from, for example, Indiana to Ohio to Kentucky to Illinois, here's how it should look:

IN>OH>KY>IL

2. **Body**. In the body of the message be specific about the information you are seeking. You should be somewhat brief, but be specific and to the point! Are you looking for proof of something (birth or death of a grandfather), or are you looking for connections to another person? You might list your phone number and address if you would like to be contacted. Of course, giving personal information on the Internet is optional. Follow your instincts with this one. If you have an unlisted number and would like it to stay that way, I wouldn't include it here. On the other hand, if your phone number is published, and you have no problem with the possibility of another researcher contacting you, by all means post it. A good reason to include your address or phone number is that e-mail addresses can change. If you change your e-mail address, without moving, other researchers will still be able to make contact with you.

Here is an example of what the body of a posting will look like:

I am looking for the parents of George Washington Melton. I know that George was born in Martin County, Indiana, on March 16, 1909, and died in Loogootee, Indiana, on September 22, 1964. He married Virginia Pershing (b. September 12, 1917— d. June 14, 1964) on November 22, 1933. I have reason to believe his father was born and raised in the same area, although I can find no records to attest to this. He married a woman by the name of Elizabeth Tomey. The information I have is from census records and I'll be happy to share information with anyone who might have links to this family tree or is researching this surname. I can be reached at the following address and phone number: xxx-xxx-xxxx. My e-mail is xxxxxxx.

Tip

Consider getting a second e-mail account through one of several free e-mail services on the Internet, then post the second e-mail. I have occasionally found online information that links to my family tree, only to discover that the e-mail address listed is no longer in use. I have made that same mistake myself, and now I always list two e-mail addresses: my current one and one provided for free by a service known as Hotmail.

I only check my Hotmail account every few weeks, but if I move, or my other e-mail address changes, online researchers will still be able to reach me. It's like having a permanent address on the Internet.

(http://www.hotmail.com)

Once you have posted your query, you can look through other people's postings to see whether you can locate any part of your family tree or connect with other researchers. Some family forums have pages and pages of postings; others have very few.

So, how do you sift through all of the postings to find one certain person? Sit up and take notice! This little trick will save you hours of research. At the bottom of each family genealogy forum page, look for Search This Forum, which has a search box beneath it. Bear in mind that you are searching *that* forum and no other—so you do not need to list the surname, just the first name of the person you are looking for. However, if you are searching for someone who *might* be in this forum, but with a different last name, like a maiden name, try searching by *that* surname instead of the one the forum specifies.

Here's an example: I am in the Melton Family Forum, searching for George Melton. By typing "George" in the forum's search engine, I might get fifty returns. If I type his wife's maiden name in the forum's search engine, I might narrow my search and get only thirty returns. Another really good way to find the best information that the search engine can provide is if I search by geographic area in a forum. If I type Daviess (county) in the Melton Family Genealogy Forum's search engine, I might retrieve information about the Melton family in Daviess County, Indiana.

Caution

When you are posting to the Internet's genealogy bulletin boards, you want to maximize the relevant responses you receive. Put a lot of thought into your post; write it out on paper before you submit it over the Internet. Make it precise, detailed, and clear. Imagine someone interviewing you about your family: What would he ask? Include every *Who? What? When?* and *Where?*

GenForum has more to offer than bulletin boards for surnames; it also has forums for countries and for states and counties in the United States. Links to these forums can be found on GenForum's home page, along with bulletin boards for general topics such as general genealogy, success stories, and record lookups.

Yes, record lookups! There are volunteers who are kind enough to do free lookups at their local courthouses. This could be a good opportunity for you to locate records from a distance. If you are going to do some research at a courthouse yourself, you could offer free lookups to help someone else.

Under specific topics on the GenForum home page, you will find the following forums: Adoption, American Indian, American Revolution, Cemetery, Church of Jesus Christ of Latter-day Saints, Civil War, Coats of Arms, Emigration, Immigrants, Inscriptions, Jewish, Medieval, Mormon, Obituaries, Photography, Tips, Rare Books, Reunion, Quaker, World War I, and World War II.

Tip

At the bottom of the GenForum home page are discussion boards for Computers and Software, where you can share technological information with other genealogists. What a valuable tool! If you have a question about a program you are using, this is a terrific place to get help, advice, and recommendations about upgrading or buying new software. This relates to your genealogy research the way a sound knowledge of tools relates to any work. If you are not using a computerized family tree program, this would be a good place to ask others for their ideas and opinions.

SECTION TWO:

E-Mail

One of the most essential elements of genealogy research is communication with other researchers. In my opinion, sharing information with others is what makes this hobby so enjoyable and rewarding. Now that correspondence on the Internet is virtually instantaneous, family researchers can meet and share information no matter how far apart they might be geographically.

Electronic mail, or e-mail, has had a remarkable impact on the genealogy community. At no other time in history have so many researchers been able to exchange such large amounts of genealogy information without making a trip to the post office or racking up expensive long-distance telephone charges.

If you already have an e-mail account, you could soon find yourself using it more for genealogy research than for any other purpose. If you do not have an e-mail account, it's very important to set yourself up with one. Even if you don't own a computer, you can have e-mail as long as you have access to a computer that is connected to the Internet—for example, at your local library or a nearby college.

The e-mail companies listed below are user-friendly; just be sure to read all the instructions as you sign up. Remember to write down your user name or ID and password. Here are three very good, free e-mail services:

1. Hotmail (see Figure 4.4) **http://www.hotmail.com**

2. Yahoo! **http://www.yahoo.com**
   (This address takes you to the Yahoo! home page, where you'll find the link to the free e-mail service near the top.)

3. Rocketmail **http://www.rocketmail.com**

Figure 4.4

The Hotmail sign up screen.

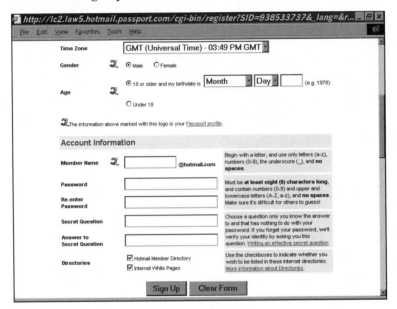

Caution

Although most e-mail programs are extremely safe, consider what type of information you are sending in your e-mail and how private you want to keep it. Most genealogy information is eventually shared and published and is therefore safe to send. Nevertheless, you might want to keep some material private—for instance, detailed information about people who are still living—and in that case e-mail can be risky. The information you send is not encrypted the way credit card information is, so your e-mail messages are not always secure.

I once received a private e-mail letter concerning child custody issues. It came to my mailbox by mistake when someone mistyped a single character in the intended e-mail address. You do not want private information in the wrong hands, so always double check the recipient line in your e-mail heading before you hit "Send."

E-mail allows even beginning genealogists to exchange information with other researchers, request data from countless resources, and actually send and receive family trees in a format called GEDCOM (Genealogical Data Communications). GEDCOM makes it possible for people who use different computerized genealogy programs to exchange information. As an example, let's say that I have my family tree typed into a computer software program such as Family Tree Maker.

While doing further research, I make contact with another person working on the same family tree. She is using a software program called Ancestry, and I have several branches of the tree that she needs. Before computers, I would have made photocopies and sent them to her by postal mail. Now, I can save the information I have in a GEDCOM format and send this to her via e-mail. It's as easy as saving a text file to a floppy disk. Here are the steps:

To send my family tree information, I first address a message to her e-mail address. I write her a short message, if I wish, and then I "attach" the GEDCOM file of my family tree to the e-mail message. When she retrieves her e-mail message and opens the GEDCOM file by double-clicking on it, her family tree program will open. The tree that I sent to her in GEDCOM will appear in Ancestry software as a file separate from her established family file.

I have had files containing as many as 4,000 names sent to me in GEDCOM. Because most genealogy programs are designed so well, they can take names from GEDCOM files and merge matching names into your files while eliminating the names of anyone who is not related to you. The software will usually ask you a question like: "Is John A. Smith the same as John Allen Smith?" Then it will let you decide what information to keep or delete as it merges files.

Another way to use e-mail is to make inquiries on genealogy message boards and forums, most of which require an e-mail address for exchanging information. First-time Internet users are sometimes apprehensive about contacting other researchers—but you can't exchange information if you don't reach out. Most genealogy Web sites, including forums, have an e-mail address at the bottom of the home page. Family researchers enjoy hearing from each other and exchanging information. If you have even one name that someone else needs, you can open a door for that person and, in the process, open one for yourself.

T i p

Make separate e-mail folders for your genealogy research. At one point I had so much e-mail coming in that it was hard to keep track of it all. The first thing I did was make separate folders for my regular e-mail and my genealogy e-mail. You might further categorize your e-mail, creating a folder for each surname. Print out your e-mails, too, and keep the hard copies filed away. It's especially important to print out correspondence containing the addresses and phone numbers of other family researchers with whom you want to stay in touch.

SECTION THREE:
Newsgroups
and Mailing Lists

A newsgroup is like a daily newspaper on one topic. There are thousands of topics covered by newsgroups on the Internet. These sites let people with the same interest exchange ideas and advice by posting messages. Topics for genealogy can be as broad as the field itself or as narrow as a specific surname.

Newsgroups provide genealogists a unique opportunity to meet and share research with other family members and with researchers who have the same surname. To be a part of a newsgroup, you will need a newsreader software program. If you have Netscape Navigator, Internet Explorer 2.0, or a more recent Web browser, the newsreader is probably already built in. If your software doesn't contain a newsreader, you can download one at the URL on the next page. Just follow the instructions for download and installation. This is a free program.

FREE AGENT NEWS READER

http://www.forteinc.com/agent/freagent.htm

Figure 4.5

Free Agent News Reader.

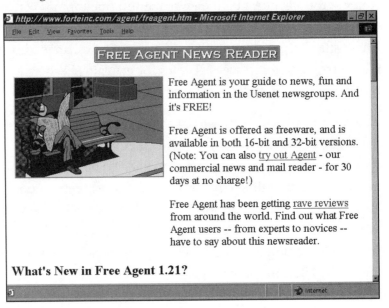

A mailing list is much like a newsgroup, but it doesn't require a newsreader. It simply "remails" all incoming mail to everyone on its subscriber lists. Each subscriber list handles a different topic, just like the newsgroups do. When you subscribe to either a newsgroup or a mailing list, you will be given three options for receiving your mail: Mail Mode, Digest Mode, or Index Mode.

◆ When you choose *Mail Mode*, the mailing list forwards each piece of mail individually.

◆ *Digest Mode* accumulates a set number of messages, say seventy-five, then sends them all at once in a single large (digest form) e-mail; its only drawback is that it can be difficult to retrieve an individual e-mail address from a particular posting.

◆ *Index Mode* will send you a daily listing of subject lines and sender lines for each posting. You can then specify the messages you want to see.

Most people prefer Digest Mode because it helps to limit a large amount of mail. If you are interested in joining a newsgroup or mailing list, a few are listed at the end of this section. Just go to the Web site and follow directions for subscribing to that particular mailing list. There are no fees to join, but you will need to set up access by specifying a password and perhaps a user ID.

C a u t i o n
The directions for subscribing to a newsgroup or mailing list must be followed to the letter. Generally, you just need to type SUBSCRIBE in all caps in the subject line of your e-mail requesting membership. To quit, type UNSUBSCRIBE in all caps in the subject line. As easy as this is, a single typo will cause your effort to fail. Newsgroup computers, like any others, recognize only the exact instructions they have been given.

Some genealogy forums are moderated, which simply means that the discussion is monitored. A moderator previews messages before they are posted, declining any that seem inappropriate or offensive. These moderated forums usually let subscribers know about this practice and might even say who does the monitoring.

FAMILY TREE MAKER'S NEWSGROUPS AND MAILING LISTS

http://www.genhomepage.com/communications

This site lists more than twenty genealogy groups, including French, German, Hispanic, Italian, and African genealogy discussion groups.

ROOTSWEB'S MAILING LISTS

http://www.rootsweb.com/~maillist

This is the biggest and best genealogy mailing list. You can search through more than 8,000 surnames represented in discussion groups. This site also covers countries, states, and counties. Read all of the information about subscribing to one of these lists. The original list has grown so big that even in Mail Mode you could receive 100 to 200 pieces of e-mail every day. Digest Mode would be far more efficient.

DEJA.COM

http://www.deja.com

F i g u r e   4 . 6

Deja.com

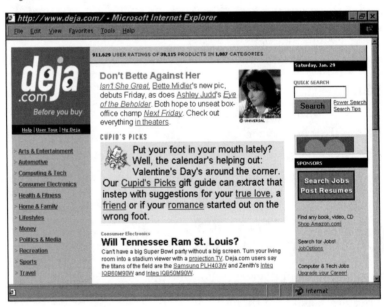

Dejanews is nothing but newsgroups! You can find discussions about anything and everything. This is a fantastic Web site for connecting with other family history researchers. If you can't find what you want, try starting a discussion of your own.

Here are just a few tips for using newsgroups and mailing lists. These tips are commonly referred to as "Netiquette."

◆ Type posts just as you would a regular letter. Avoid using all caps, which looks like "screaming."

◆ Make your subject line a brief, to-the-point description of your post.

◆ In your message, keep to the point and discuss only one subject at a time.

◆ Consider privacy. You never know who will read your posts. On matters you don't want to make public, contact the relevant people directly through e-mail, or use postal mail if something is truly sensitive.

◆ Make your queries as specific as possible. Ask for information about a particular person, not just a surname.

◆ If you can answer someone else's post, do so in a post if it could benefit the rest of the discussion group. Otherwise, e-mail the person directly.

Genealogy
Lessons Online

Family researchers often get stumped in their search for a date, place, or other important detail. Whether you are an expert or a newcomer to genealogy, you can benefit from free online genealogy lessons. Some people need basic instruction, while others just need to brush up on skills or find a new perspective. Listed here are two really great Web sites for online traditional genealogy classes. Although these classes will cover research via the Internet, their primary focus is to explain how to research genealogy through your local courthouse or genealogy library. And yes—*the lessons are free.*

FAMILY TREE MAKER'S
GENEALOGY LESSONS ONLINE

http://www.familytreemaker.com/university.html

Family Tree Maker's Online Genealogy Lessons provide the necessary tools to conduct a step-by-step family history search. The courses, written by experts, cover every aspect of both traditional and online research. The lessons are separated into categories so that you can start at the beginning or jump in to any area in which you have questions. This is an excellent learning tool!

ANCESTRY'S GENEALOGY LESSONS ONLINE

http://www.ancestry.com/learn/start/

Figure 4.7

Ancestry's Genealogy Lessons Online.

Ancestry's gift to the Internet is not only online genealogy lessons, but a Dear Abby of sorts to the genealogy community. This "Abby" is Pat Isaacs Richley, better known as "Dear Myrtle." She has a comfortable way of explaining even the most complicated things. All of her articles are archived and easily accessible. She answers everything from questions about complex privacy issues to the most basic questions that a beginning genealogist might ask.

ANCESTRY CORNER

http://www.ancestrycorner.com

This is not affiliated with the Ancestry site mentioned in the last Web site. Although Ancestry Corner is a small business that offers genealogy books and CD-ROMs for sale, it also has free online forms for genealogy research. You can find free online forms at other genealogy Web sites like Family Tree Maker and Ancestry. The forms at this site have no advertising on them, and they are ready to print out and take with you on your next trip to a courthouse or cemetery. Here are a few of the forms you can obtain at this site: Four Generation Ancestor Chart, Cemetery Abstract Chart, Marriage Abstract Chart, and Census History Form for Individuals.

Figure 4.8
Free Cemetery Log form retrieved from Ancestry Corner.

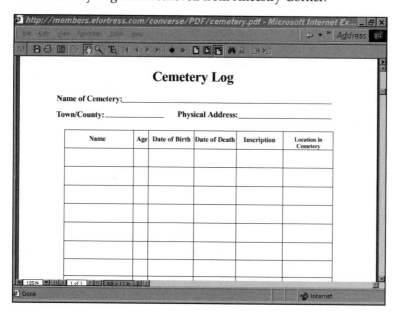

SECTION FIVE:
Last Words

This last step of this book is *Connecting Online.* The human connection you make with family members and other researchers is presumably the most gratifying reason to begin your own family history project. In the past, genealogy has been a hobby that required some travel, phone bills, and a lot of time. Now, thanks to the Internet, family history research has become an inexpensive and enjoyable hobby for millions. People who work during the day don't have to worry about when the courthouses or libraries will be open, because many records can be ordered online or viewed for free, at the researcher's convenience. With access to the Internet, genealogists can sift through online records as easily at 1 a.m. as at 1 p.m.

Here's a brief outline for conducting your own genealogy research on and off the Internet, *covering all of the bases.*

1. Gather and organize as much information as you can about your family history before beginning your research on the Internet. Start with yourself and others in your generation, then work back in time.

2. Become familiar with your computer's Web browser. Make good use of all of your computer's features, like using the Find function within your Web browser.

3. Put your family genealogy data into a family tree software program of your choice. Back up the data often and print out hard copies of your work.

4. If you choose the surname(s) that you want to research, begin with the earliest record you have for each surname.

5. Search within comprehensive databases like Ancestry, Family Tree Maker, Family Search, U.S. GenWeb, and RootsWeb. Perform advanced searches using each Web site's search engine. Search smart!

6. Post to forums like GenForum. Search within surname forums for connections to family trees and also to other researchers.

7. Subscribe to a mailing list. Consider setting up a free e-mail account online if you want a permanent e-mail address to post online or are worried about getting too much incoming e-mail to your home account.

8. Visit your state's archives online.

9. Delve into ship lists, census records, Social Security Death Index (SSDI), military records, maps and land records online.

10. Write or e-mail requests for information from reference Web sites such as genealogy libraries or courthouses.

11. Take genealogy lessons online for free.

12. Visit a genealogy library in your area. Using the online links to genealogy libraries will help you plan your visit.

13. After you have thoroughly searched all of the Web sites recommended here, go back and search again. Remember that the Internet is an ever-changing environment, with new genealogy information being added every day.

14. Your future goals might include setting up a Web page to display your findings. You can submit your tree to Ancestry or Family Tree Maker and it will publish your tree online. When you begin to share your knowledge with others, you will also make connections that you couldn't find before.

Never give up!

"There is no reason anyone would want a computer in their home."

—Ken Olson, founder and president
of Digital Equipment Corporation, 1977

Appendixes

APPENDIX A
Glossary

Archive—A set of historic records and documents preserved by a government, organization, or institution; the place in which such records are kept.

Attachment—A file or program that is sent with, but not in the body of, an e-mail message.

Bulletin board—An Internet site where people with similar interests post news and ask questions pertaining to a particular subject.

CD (or **CD-ROM**)—Compact disc (with) read-only memory.

Chat—Online, real-time correspondence with other network users; an instantaneous electronic conversation.

Cookie—A marker, or piece of information, that a Web site might place on your computer so that it can recognize you the next time you visit that Web site.

Database—A large collection of records or other information put into a computerized format and indexed for easy retrieval.

Digest Mode—A method of receiving mail from a mailing list, in which messages accumulate to a set number and are then forwarded to subscribers in a single large e-mail.

Download—The transfer of a file from one computer to another, usually from a large computer to a smaller one.

Emigration—The act of moving away from one country or region to live in another.

E-mail—Electronic mail, which can be sent from one computer to another as long as each has the necessary software. E-mail can include text, pictures, or computer programs.

Family History Centers—Genealogy libraries run by the Church of Jesus Christ of Latter-day Saints, which house not only local but national and international information.

Forum—An online community bulletin board where one can find or post information on general or highly specific topics.

FTP—File Transfer Protocol, a program that transfers files from one computer to another. FTP is commonly used to download programs and other data from the Internet.

GEDCOM—Genealogical Data Communications, a program that allows researchers using different genealogy software programs to exchange files without having to retype or reformat them.

Home page—The opening page, or home base, of a Web site, which usually outlines the site's services and data.

HTML—Hypertext Markup Language, the computer programming language that is used to write pages for the World Wide Web.

Hyperlink—A means of moving from one Web page or Web site to another. A hyperlink usually appears on the computer screen as a word, phrase or Web address highlighted in blue or another color. To move to the indicated new location, the user clicks on the highlighted material.

Immigration—The act of moving into a new country.

Index Mode—A method of receiving mail from a mailing list, in which a list of each day's messages is sent to subscribers using only the subject and sender lines. The recipient can then choose which messages to read in full.

Internet—A massive collection of data placed online, for worldwide public use, by government agencies, public and private organizations, businesses, universities, libraries, and individuals; the network of all computers, worldwide, capable of accessing or posting the data.

Link—See *Hyperlink*.

Mailing list—An online service that e-mails subscribers news, information, and messages relating to a given topic.

Mail Mode—A method of receiving mail from a mailing list, in which each piece of mail is forwarded to subscribers individually.

Moderator—One who reviews messages for format, relevance, and appropriateness before allowing them to be posted on a forum.

Newsgroup—An online service that collects postings on a given topic and sends news and information to subscribers via e-mail.

Search engine—An online service that scans the World Wide Web or individual Web sites for files containing keywords typed in by the user.

Searchable database—A large file of information organized so that it can be scanned by a search engine.

Snail mail—Traditional postal mail delivery, so called because it is slow in comparison to electronic mail (e-mail).

Soundex—A method of indexing any surname, regardless of spelling variations, using a code of one letter and three numbers.

Surname—A person's last name (family name).

Upload—The transfer of a file or other information from one computer to another one.

URL—Uniform Resource Locator; the computer address for a given Web site.

Vital records—Official records showing dates, places, and times of life events such as births, deaths, and marriages.

Web browser—A program that allows users to view and move about in the Internet. Internet Explorer and Netscape Navigator are the two most common Web browsers.

Web page—A document available for viewing on the Internet. The page is usually reached through a connecting Web site.

Web site—An Internet location (reached via a URL) at which you can find information on an organization or topic, along with links to other, related Web pages or sites.

World Wide Web (www)—A "global switchboard," that covers the Internet, linking all Web sites.

APPENDIX B

Genealogy Terms

Abstract—A summary of documents like deeds and wills.

Administration (of estate)—Legally dividing and distributing an estate to the proper heirs.

Administrator (of estate)—Person appointed to oversee the management and distribution of an estate among the heirs.

Administratrix—A female administrator of an estate.

Affidavit—A written statement which has been sworn to before the proper authority.

Alien—Foreigner.

Ancestor—A person from whom you are descended.

Ancestry—A person's lineage.

Apprentice—A person bound by service to another person, by legal agreement, for a specified period of time to learn an art or trade.

Appurtenance—That which belongs to something else, such as a right of way.

Archives—Records belonging to a government, organization, or institution; place where records are stored.

Attest—To declare by signature or oath.

Banns—Public announcement of intended marriage.

Beneficiary—One who receives benefit of trust or property.

Bequeath—To give personal property to a person in a will.

Bond—A legally binding agreement to perform certain duties or requiring payment on or before a given date.

Bounty Land—Land granted as a reward for those who enlisted in service of the military.

Census—An official counting of citizens.

Chattel—Personal property, which can include animate as well as inanimate properties.

Christen—To receive or initiate into the church by baptism.

Circa—About, near, or approximate, usually referring to a date.

Codicil—Addition to a will.

Collateral Ancestor—Belonging to the same ancestral stock but not in direct line of descent, as opposed to lineal such as aunts, uncles and cousins.

Common Ancestor—Ancestor shared by any two people.

Consanguinity—Blood relationship.

Consort—Usually, a wife whose husband is living.

Conveyances—Deeds.

Deceased—Dead.

Decedent—A deceased person.

Declaration of Intention—First paper, sworn to and filed in court, by an alien stating that he wants to become a citizen.

Deed—A document by which title in real property is transferred from one party to another.

Deposition—A testifying or testimony taken down in writing and given under oath in reply to interrogatories, before a competent officer, to replace the oral testimony of a witness.

Descendant—Offspring of a person.

Devisee—One to whom property is given in a will.

Devisor—One who gives property in a will.

Dissenter—One who did not belong to the established church.

District Land Office Plat Book—Books containing the maps that show the location of land patentees.

District Land Office Tract Book—Books which list individual entries by range and township.

Dower—Legal right or share which a wife acquired by marriage in the real estate of her husband, allotted to her after his death for her lifetime or until her remarriage.

Emigrant—One leaving a country and moving to another.

Enumeration—Listing or counting people, like the census.

Epitaph—An inscription on or at a tomb or grave in memory of the one buried there.

Escheat—The reversion of property to the state when there are no qualified heirs.

Estate—All property and debts belonging to a person.

Et Al—Latin for "and others."

Et Ux—Latin for "and wife."

Et Uxor—Latin for "and his wife." Sometimes written simply Et Ux.

Executor—A man appointed in a will to carry out the provisions of that will.

Executrix—A woman appointed in a will to carry out the provisions of that will.

Fee—An estate of inheritance in land, being either fee simple or fee tail.

Fee Simple—An absolute ownership without restriction.

Fee Tail—An estate of inheritance limited to the lineal descendant heirs of a person.

Genealogy—Study of family history.

Grantee—One who buys property or receives a grant.

Grantor—One who sells property or makes a grant.

Guardian—Person appointed to care for and manage property of a minor orphan or an adult incompetent of managing his own affairs.

Heirs—Those legally granted in a will to inherit property from another.

Holographic Will—Will written entirely in the testator's own handwriting.

Homestead Act—Law passed by Congress in 1862 allowing a head of a family to obtain title to 160 acres of public land after clearing and improving it for five years.

Immigrant—One moving into a country from another.

Indenture—A contract which was originally made in two parts by tearing a single sheet across the middle in a jagged line so that the two parts may later be matched together.

Indentured Servant—A servant bound, by choice, into service of another person for a specified number of years. Often this was done in return for transportation to this country.

Instant—Pertaining to the current month. Usually an abbreviated term, "inst."

Intestate—One who dies without a will.

Issue—Offspring; children; lineal descendants of a common ancestor.

Lease—Similar to a rental agreement, creating a landlord-and-tenant situation.

Legacy—Property or money left to someone in a will.

Lien—A claim against property as security for payment of a debt.

Lineage—A line of direct descendants from a specific ancestor.

Lineal—A direct line of ancestors or descendants.

Measurements—
  Link—7.92 inches
  Chain—4 rods, or 100 links, or 66 feet
  Square Chain—16 poles
  Pole—625 square links
  Furlong—1,000 links or 660 feet
  Rod—5 1/2 yards, or 25 links, or 16 1/2 ft (also known as a perch or pole)
  Rood—From 5 1/2 yards to 8 yards
  Acre—43,560 square ft, or 160 square rods, or 10 square chains
  Mile—80 chains
  Square mile—640 acres

Microfiche—Sheet of microfilm which contains rows of pages in a greatly reduced format.

Microfilm—Film on which documents are photographed and greatly reduced in size.

Migrant—Person, in search of work, who moves from place to place.

Mortality Schedules—An enumeration, conducted by the bureaus of census, of people who died during the year prior to June 1 of 1850, 1860, 1870, and 1880 in each state of the United States, conducted by the Bureau of Census.

Necrology—Listing or record of persons who have died recently.

Nee—Used to identify a woman's maiden name.

Probate—Legal process of determining that a will is valid before authorizing distribution of the estate, appointing someone to administer an intestate estate, and overseeing the settlements of estates.

Passenger List—A ship's list of passengers, usually referring to those ships arriving in the U.S. from Europe.

Patent—Grant of land from a government to an individual.

Paternal—Related through one's father.

Patriot—A person who supports the best interests of his country.

Pedigree—A person's family tree or lineage.

Poll—A list or record of people.

Posterity—Descendants.

Power of Attorney—When a person appoints another to act in his behalf.

Pre-emotion Rights—Right given by the federal government to citizens to buy a quarter section of land or less.

Probate—Having to do with wills and the administration of estates.

Progenitor—A direct ancestor.

Progeny—Descendants of a common ancestor.

Proved Will—A will established as genuine by probate court.

Provost—A person appointed to preside over something.

Public Domain—Land owned by the government.

Quitclaim—A deed conveying the interest of the party at that time.

Rector—A clergyman; the ruler or governor of a country.

Relict—Surviving spouse when one has died.

Republic—Government in which supreme authority lies with the people or their elected representatives.

Shaker—Member of a religious group formed in 1747 which practiced communal living and celibacy.

Sic—Latin meaning *thus*; copied exactly as the original reads.

Sponsor—A bondsman.

Statute—Law.

Surname—Family name or last name.

Territory—Area of land (not a state) owned by the United States.

Testamentary—Pertaining to a will.

Testate—A person who dies leaving a valid will.

Testator—A person who makes a valid will before his death.

Tithable—Taxable.

Tithe—Money due as a tax for support of the clergy or church.

Township—A division of U.S. public land that contained 36 sections, or 36 square miles. Also a subdivision of the county in many Northeastern and Midwestern states of the U.S.

Tradition—The handing down of statements, beliefs, legends, customs, genealogies, etc. from generation to generation, especially by word of mouth.

Transcribe—To make a handwritten copy.

Ultimo—In the month before this one.

Verbatim—Word for word; in the same words; verbally.

Vital Records—Records of birth, death, marriage or divorce.

Vital Statistics—Data dealing with birth, death, marriage or divorce.

Ward—The legal division of a city for election purposes.

Will—Document declaring how a person wants his property divided after his death.

Witness—One who is present at a transaction, such as a sale of land or signing of a will, who can testify or affirm that it actually took place.

Yeoman—A farmer who owns his land.

Relationship Abbreviations

Here are some relationship abbreviations used in genealogy research. You will see these abbreviations primarily in census records.

A	Aunt
AdD	Adopted Daughter
AdS	Adopted Son
At	Attendant
B	Brother
BL	Brother-in-law
Bo	Boarder
C	Cousin
D	Daughter
F	Father
FB	Foster Brother
FF	Foster Father
FL	Father-in-law
FM	Foster Mother
Fsi	Foster Sister
GA	Great-Aunt
GD	Granddaughter

GF	Grandfather
GGF	Great-Grandfather
GGGF	Great-Great-Grandfather
GGGM	Great-Great-Grandmother
GGM	Great-Grandmother
GM	Grandmother
Gni	Grandniece
GS	Grandson
GU	Great-Uncle
Hh	Hired hand
I	Inmate
L	Lodger
M	Mother
ML	Mother-in-law
N	Nephew
Ni	Niece
Nu	Nurse
O	Officer
P	Patient
Pr	Prisoner
Pri	Principal
Pu	Pupil
R	Roomer

S	Son
SB	Stepbrother
SBL	Stepbrother-in-law
Se	Servant
SF	Stepfather
SFL	Stepfather-in-law
Si	Sister
SiL	Sister-in-law
SL	Son-in-law
SM	Stepmother
SML	Stepmother-in-law
SS	Stepson
Ssi	Stepsister
SSiL	Stepsister-in-law
SSL	Stepson-in-law
Su	Superintendent
U	Uncle
W	Wife
Wa	Warden

Occupations

When doing genealogy research, one problem people encounter is the need to decipher the meanings of outdated words. To better understand census records and other recorded occupations, refer to this list of meanings. Notice that many of these occupations have since become common surnames!

Accomptant—Accountant

Almoner—A philanthropist; a person who gives to the needy

Amanuensis—Stenographer or secretary

Artificer—A soldier mechanic

Bailie—Bailiff

Baxter—Baker

Bluestocking—Female writer or intellectual

Boniface—An innkeeper

Brazier—One who works with brass

Brewster—Beer manufacturer

Brightsmith—Metal worker

Burgomaster—Mayor

Caulker—One who fills up cracks (in ships or windows)

Chaisemaker—Carriage maker

Chandler—Dealer or trader, usually referring to one who sells candles or a grocery retailer

Chiffonnier—Wig maker

Clark—Clerk

Clerk—Clergyman

Clicker—One who makes eyelet holes in boots using a machine which clicked

Cohen—Priest

Collier—Coal miner

Colporteur—Book peddler

Cooper—One who makes or repairs vessels such as casks, barrels, tubs, etc.

Costermonger—Fruit and vegetable peddler

Crocker—Potter

Crowner—Coroner

Currier—One who tans leather by incorporating oil or grease

Docker—Dock worker who loads and unloads cargo

Dowser—One who finds water using a rod or witching stick

Draper—A dealer in dry goods

Drayman—One who drives a strong cart without fixed sides for carrying heavy loads

Dresser—A surgeon's assistant in a hospital

Drover—One who drives cattle, sheep, etc. to market

Duffer—Peddler

Factor—One who acts or transacts business for another

Farrier—A blacksmith, one who shoes horses

Fell monger—One who removes hair or wool from hides for leather making

Fletcher—One who makes bows and arrows

Fuller—One who cleans and finishes cloth

Gaoler—A jailer

Glazier—Window glassman

Hacker—Maker of hoes

Hatcheler—One who combs out or carded flax

Haymonger—Dealer in hay

Hayward—Keeper of fences

Higgler—Itinerant peddler

Hillier—Roof tiler

Hind—A farm laborer

Hostler—A groom who takes care of horses, often at an inn

Hooker—Reaper

Hooper—One who makes hoops for casks and barrels

Huckster—Seller of small wares

Husbandman—A farmer who cultivates the land

Jagger—Fish peddler

Journeyman—One who had served his apprenticeship and mastered his craft, not bound to serve a master, but hired by the day

Joyner/Joiner—A skilled carpenter

Kempster—Wool comber

Lardner—Keeper of the cupboard

Lavender—Washer woman

Lederer—Leather maker

Leech—Physician

Longshoreman—Stevedore

Lormer—Maker of horse gear

Malender—Farmer

Maltster—Brewer

Manciple—A steward

Mason—Bricklayer

Mintmaster—One who issues local currency

Monger—Seller of goods

Muleskinner—Teamster

Neatherder—One who herds cows

Ordinary Keeper—Innkeeper with fixed prices

Peregrinator—Itinerant, wanderer

Peruker—A wig maker

Pettifogger—A shyster lawyer

Pigman—Crockery dealer

Plumber—One who applies sheet lead for roofing and set lead frames for plain or stained glass windows

Porter—Door keeper

Puddler—Wrought iron worker

Quarrier—Quarry worker

Rattlewatch—Town watchman

Ripper—Seller of fish

Roper—Maker of rope or nets

Saddler—One who makes, repairs, or sells saddles or other furnishings for horses

Sawbones—Physician

Sawyer—Carpenter

Schumacker—Shoemaker

Scribler—A minor or worthless author

Scrivener—Professional or public copyist or writer; notary public

Scrutiner—Election judge

Shrieve—Sheriff

Slater—Roofer

Slopseller—Seller of ready-made clothes

Snobscat/Snob—One who repairs shoes

Sorter—Tailor

Spinster—A woman who spins; an unmarried woman

Spurrer—Maker of spurs

Squire—Farm owner; justice of peace

Supercargo—Officer on merchant ship who is in charge of cargo

Tanner—One who tans (cures) animal hides into leather

Tapley—One who puts the tap in an ale cask

Tasker—Reaper

Teamster—One who drives a team for hauling

Thatcher—Roofer

Tide waiter—Customs inspector

Tinker—A traveling tin pot and pan seller and repairman

Tipstaff—Policeman

Travers—Toll bridge collector

Tucker—Cleaner of cloth goods

Turner—A person who turns wood on a lathe into spindles

Victualer—A tavern keeper, or one who provides an army, navy, or ship with food supplies

Vulcan—Blacksmith

Wagoner—Teamster not for hire

Wainwright—Wagon maker

Waiter—Customs officer

Webster—Operator of looms

Wharfinger—Owner of a wharf

Wheelwright—One who makes or repairs wheels

Whitesmith—Tinsmith; worker of iron who finishes or polishes the work

Whitewing—Street sweeper

Wright—Workman, especially a construction worker

Yeoman—Farmer who owns his own land

Historical Epidemics of the Last 350 Years

Anyone who has done genealogy research will tell you that one of the most frustrating things is locating someone whom you know existed but can find no trace of. Your written or oral family history may tell of someone who lived, but then suddenly vanished from the public record system.

Census schedules are a wonderful source for tracking family births, marriages, and movements from one area to another, but census records cannot tell the whole story. If you are at a brick wall in research, check the dates here and consider the possibility that the ancestor may have succumbed to an epidemic or even moved away from the region affected by the epidemic. Here are some major epidemics that have plagued our ancestors for the last 350 years.

Year	Location	Epidemic
1657	Boston	Measles
1687	Boston	Measles
1690	New York	Yellow Fever
1713	Boston	Measles
1729	Boston	Measles
1732-33	Worldwide	Influenza
1738	South Carolina	Smallpox
1739-40	Boston	Measles

Year	Location	Epidemic
1747	Conn, N.Y., Pa., S.C.	Measles
1759	N. America [areas inhabited by white people]	Measles
1761	N. America and West Indies	Influenza
1772	N. America	Measles
1775	N. America [especially hard in the N.E.]	Epidemic Unknown
1775-76	Worldwide [one of the worst epidemics]	Influenza
1783	Dover, Delaware [extremely fatal]	Bilious Disorder
1788	Philadelphia and New York	Measles
1793	Vermont	a "putrid" fever and Influenza
1793	Virginia [killed 500 in 5 counties in 4 weeks]	Influenza
1793	Philadelphia [one of the worst epidemics]	Yellow Fever
1793	Harrisburg, Pa. [many unexplained deaths]	Unknown
1793	Middletown, Pa. [many unexplained deaths]	Unknown
1794	Philadelphia	Yellow Fever
1796-97	Philadelphia	Yellow Fever

Year	Location	Epidemic
1798	Philadelphia [one of the worst epidemics]	Yellow Fever
1803	New York	Yellow Fever
1820-23	Nationwide [starts at Schuylkill River and spreads]	"Fever"
1831-32	Nationwide [brought by English emigrants]	Asiatic Cholera
1832	New York City and other major cities	Cholera
1833	Columbus, Ohio	Cholera
1834	New York City	Cholera
1837	Philadelphia	Typhus
1841	Nationwide [especially severe in the South]	Yellow Fever
1847	New Orleans	Yellow Fever
1847-48	Worldwide	Influenza
1848-49	North America	Cholera
1849	New York	Cholera
1850	Nationwide	Yellow Fever
1850-51	North America	Influenza
1851	Coles Co., Illinois, The Great Plains, and Missouri	Cholera
1852	Nationwide [New Orleans—8,000 die in one summer]	Yellow Fever

Year	Location	Epidemic
1855	Nationwide [many parts]	Yellow Fever
1857-59	Worldwide [one of the greatest epidemics]	Influenza
1860-61	Pennsylvania	Smallpox
1865-73	Philadelphia, New York, Boston, New Orleans	Smallpox
1865-73	Baltimore, Memphis, Washington D.C.	Cholera
1865-73	A series of recurring epidemics	Typhus, Typhoid, Scarlet Fever, Yellow Fever
1873-75	N. America and Europe	Influenza
1878	New Orleans [last great epidemic]	Yellow Fever
1885	Plymouth, Pa.	Typhoid
1886	Jacksonville, Fla.	Yellow Fever
1918	Worldwide*	Influenza

*More people were hospitalized in World War I from this epidemic than from wounds. U.S. Army training camps became death camps, with an 80% death rate in some camps. More people died from the influenza epidemic than died in all of the wars of this century. Death was rapid. Many fell ill and died the same day.

Index

NOTE: Italicized page numbers refer to illustrations, tips, notes, or caution boxes. A glossary precedes this index.

A

B

C

D

E

F

G

H

I

J

K

L

M

N

O

P

Q

R

S

🌿 T

U

V

W

Y

CREATING PAINT SHOP PRO WEB GRAPHICS

Price: $44.99
ISBN: 0-9662889-0-4
Pages: 384
Author: Andy Shafran

Full Color

Foreword by
Chris Anderson,
VP of Marketing,
Jasc Software

Highlights

Sixteen focused chapters teach you how to understand layers, special effects, plug-ins, and other important Paint Shop Pro features

Integrates with a comprehensive Web site that contains updated information, complete examples, and frequently asked questions

Detailed Web-specific topics such as transparency, animation, Web art, digital photography, scanners, and more

SCANNER SOLUTIONS

Price: $29.95
ISBN: 0-9662889-7-1
Pages: 320
Author: Winston Steward

• Full Color
• Tabbed Sections
• Index for easy use

Highlights

• Shows readers how to use their scanners for personal entertainment, in their home office, and in conjunction with the Internet

• Describes how to purchase and install scanners, specific hardware and software performance tips, and how to use the scanner as an important piece of office equipment

• Discusses photo editing, graphic design, desktop publishing, OCR, saving and archiving, and retrieving files

DIGITAL CAMERA SOLUTIONS
EDIT, PRINT & USE YOUR DIGITAL PHOTOS EFFECTIVELY

Price: $29.95
ISBN: 0-9662889-6-3
Pages: 368
Author: Gregory Georges

Full Color

Tabbed Sections

Index for easy use

Highlights

Teaches readers how to edit digital images, prepare them for the Internet, and print them in a high quality format

Contains dozens of examples and projects to use with any type or brand of digital camera

Focuses on mastering digital camera software and photo manipulation techniques

EBAY ONLINE AUCTIONS

Price: $14.95
ISBN: 0-9662889-4-7
Pages: 240
Author: Neil J. Salkind

• Glossary
• Question and Answer format

Highlights

• Explains the concepts behind how eBay works

• Fully explains the bidding, buying, and selling process for items, handling payment, and obtaining the auctioned items

• Describes the different types of auctions, options available for bidders and sellers, and limitations of each format

Order Form

Postal Orders:
  Muska & Lipman Publishing
  2645 Erie Avenue, Suite 41
  Cincinnati, Ohio 45208

On-Line Orders or more information:
  http://www.muskalipman.com
Fax Orders:
  (513) 924-9333

Title/ISBN	Price/Cost

Genealogy Basics Online
1-9296850-0-9
  Quantity _____

  × $24.95

  Total Cost _____

eBay Online Auctions
0-9662889-4-7
  Quantity _____

  × $14.95

  Total Cost _____

Creating Paint Shop Pro Web Graphics
0-9662889-0-4
  Quantity _____
  × $44.99

  Total Cost _____

Title/ISBN	Price/Cost

Digital Camera Solutions
0-9662889-6-3
  Quantity _____

  × $29.95

  Total Cost _____

Scanner Solutions
0-9662889-7-1
  Quantity _____

  × $29.95

  Total Cost _____

Subtotal _____

Sales Tax _____
(please add 6% for books
shipped to Ohio addresses)

Shipping _____
($4.00 for the first book,
$2.00 each additional book)

TOTAL PAYMENT ENCLOSED _____

Ship to:
  Company _____

  Name _____

  Address _____

  City _____ State _____ Zip _____ Country _____

Educational facilities, companies, and organizations interested in multiple copies of these books should contact the publisher for quantity discount information. Training manuals, CD-ROMs, electronic versions, and portions of these books are also available individually or can be tailored for specific needs.

Thank you for your order.